Miriam ... To say th[?] [?] [?]

yours is an understatement.

with love

Camilla

Fans

Fans

A Collector's Guide

Nancy Armstrong

SOUVENIR PRESS

First published 1984 by Souvenir Press Ltd,
43 Great Russell Street, London WC1B 3PA
and simultaneously in Canada

ISBN 0 285 62591 8

Filmset and printed in Great Britain by
BAS Printers Limited,
Over Wallop, Hampshire

Contents

For Peter, my dearly loved and eldest son.

List of Illustrations

COLOUR PLATES

BLACK AND WHITE PHOTOGRAPHS

Acknowledgements

Many people in the 'fan world' are generous to a fault with their help and encouragement. I could not have written this book (or my previous one) without the aid of the following:

Hélène Alexander, Felicity Barnett, Sam Farr, Madeleine Ginsburg, Grace Grayson, the late Bertha de Vere Green, Peter Greenhalgh, Avril Hart, Milne Henderson, Betty Hodgkinson, Pamela Hudson, Dr. Richard Illing, Neville Iröns, Prue Lachelin, John Lawson, Margaret Little, Santina Levey, Miss Lintott, Michel Maignan, Susan Mayor, Jane Mitchell, Esther Oldham, the Rt Hon Lord Oranmore and Browne, Geraldine Pember, the late Eleanor Robinson, Anne, Countess of Rosse, Larry Salmon, Miss Smedley, Sheila Smith, the staff of the Spanish Institute, Katy Talati, Edward Thornton-Vincent, Georgette Tilley, Gillian Troche, Anthony Vaughan, Ian Venture and Martin Willcocks.

1 Collecting Fans

We feel attracted to fans not simply because they are old—not even because they are necessarily beautiful. Their most magnetic appeal comes from the glimpses they give us into the lives people lived long before we were born. For an antique fan should not be an object simply to possess and invest in, but a chink in the door of the past, a whisper through a bygone age that thrills the collector like a signal from a distant planet. Historians may unfold for us the panorama of great events without wringing out a single tear; a lonely Victorian child's fan can fill us with tender amazement. It is just because this small fan appears to be so trivial, and so everyday, that the insight we can gain from it gives it such poignancy. Fans seem to have a life of their own: they are intensely personal because the majority have been owned and used. Writers about fans today are constantly driven by the questions, 'When was it made? Why? Who used it? Which was its country of origin? How was it made?' Following up the answers to these questions provides the collector with a whole new world of sheer delight.

There has been a sudden and dramatic re-awakening of interest in the subject of fans during the past ten years. Since the early 1970s, by pure coincidence, several books on the subject have come onto the market. They are, in date order:

A Collector's History of Fans (1974)
A Collector's Guide to Fans over the Ages (1975)
The Fan (1976)
Fans from the East (1978)
The Book of Fans (1978)
Collecting Fans (1980)
Fans from Imperial China (1982)
Fans from Imperial Japan (1982)

These books were all written in English and have all contributed a great deal towards a deeper knowledge about fans: if mistakes have been made they were not deliberate or dishonest, for in this new field we have all progressed and matured by error. No one has exclusive knowledge, more research is being done all the time on different aspects of fans, and it becomes more and more evident that they are inescapably tied in with social history.

Until 1974 many people felt that fans meant 'frivolous ladies in fashionable dress semaphoring prospective suitors'. To a certain extent this might have been so—but only for a very short period of time. On the whole the fan, the fly-whisk and the umbrella were symbols of social position which, in the majority of cases, meant that they were used by men.

The word 'fan', therefore, is a very loose term overall, encompassing many different things, and more and more books are necessary to explore the wide variety of specialist categories which have emerged. Serious collectors, academics and historians now seem to be concentrating on the following main themes:

1 Oriental fans for the home market
2 Export fans from the Orient
3 Ethnographical fans
4 Ceremonial and religious fans
5 Historical fans
6 European fans *c* 1650–*c* 1930
7 Modern fans

In the past collectors were free to make their choice between these categories; today the value of a fan has sharpened so much that it would be senseless and untrue to suggest that a new collector has all that much choice, especially with a limited pocket.

Obviously historical fans in museums will stay there, and so will most religious fans in temples (although, naturally, the social historian can write them up very fully). If the new collector has the nerve to back his or her own judgement, the area least explored today is that of ethnography; otherwise I would suggest buying some unmounted Oriental fan-leaf that caught the eye. It is always wisest to buy the best you can afford; quality is a sound investment, and much Oriental art is still undervalued in Europe. However, it must be remembered that ethnographical fans are not sold as such in auction sales, but under the section 'African works of Art', etc., and Oriental fan-leaves are sold within 'Oriental Painting' sales.

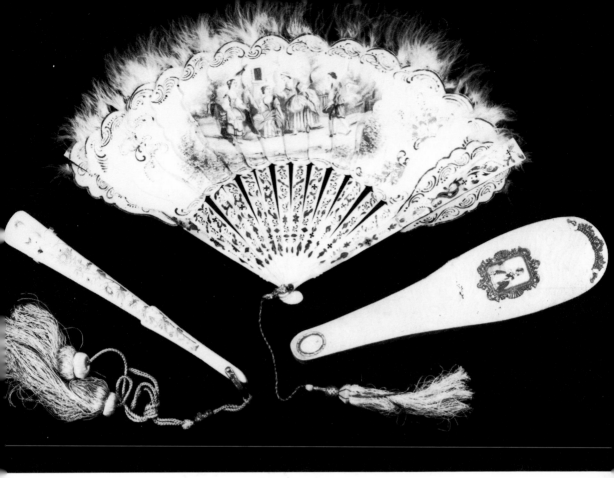

1. Left: a closed fan, showing the guard with shibayama inlay. Possibly mid-19th century. Japanese. 11" : 28cms. Centre and right: the leaf painted with a scene from 18th century life but in the 19th century manner, each leaf edged with maribou feathers, mounted on pierced and gilded mother-of-pearl sticks. Possibly French, made for the Spanish market. c 1860. 11" : 29 cms, shown with its original case. By courtesy of Bonhams, Knightsbridge.

In Category 1 (above) only artistic content and merit should be considered. In Category 3 it is extremely important to have a full provenance. In Category 6 craft comes before art in the main and, at best, is an amalgam of the two. This is the area from which most new collectors enthusiastically gather their fans and where one can begin extremely modestly. Then, in time, a personal statement can be made which reflects either the state of one's purse or one's taste.

The most important aspect of collecting is that each major purchase (it cannot happen every time) should have an impeccable provenance: it is pointless to boast that your fan was once owned by Marie Antoinette or was painted by Michelangelo unless there is positive written proof—word of mouth does *not* count.

A fan known to have been in any Royal hands (almost any country, almost any period) is generally much more valuable than it actually warrants; the same applies, to a lesser degree, to fans once owned by people in the theatre, or by artists or authors. Fans bought from the sale of a well-known collection should always keep their sale tags on them, together with the sale catalogue for proof.

The best advice that one can give to prospective collectors is to buy what they really like and to pay as much as they can afford at the time for one fan, rather than buying a selection for the same price—for quality costs money and you have to live with your enthusiasm every day. Nothing is more soul-destroying than to hear of people buying what they do not really care for, purely as an investment, and then

2. Italian fan, the black kid leaf painted with Adonis surprising the sleeping Venus with an audience of putti; mounted on ivory sticks painted in the chinoiserie manner. c 1700. 10½″: 26.5 cms. By courtesy of Bonhams, Knightsbridge.

putting the purchase away until it can be sold at a profit—why not just buy stocks and shares?

Some people feel that brand new collectors should buy some exceptionally cheap fans (say about five) merely as a starting point: to get the feel of them, learn about them, handle them and compare them with illustrations in the standard books. Then, when they feel confident enough, they should branch out into a chosen field and throw the original five away . . . or sell them.

Most new collectors set out with little or no idea of where their preferences lie and think of fans as being merely charming and colourful adjuncts to dress. Some are brought into the collecting field because they discovered a cache of fans in the dressing-up box, or because their grandmother left them a treasured marriage fan which she, in turn, inherited from Victorian times. Gradually, as the collection grows, so does one's knowledge, until suddenly a shape appears to the collection. That is the time to sell or exchange the unworthy and start to specialise. A guide to both expensive and cheap fans is tabled below:

Expensive fans of top quality
>Seventeenth century varnished fans
>Eighteenth century cabriolet fans
>Eighteenth century lace fans
>Oriental fans for the home market
>Oriental fans leaves
>Mask or Domino fans
>Mica fans
>Fans with real gemstones
>Eighteenth century commemorative fans
>Some ethnographical fans
>Gut fans

Cheaper fans are found amongst the following
>Advertising fans
>Small wooden brisé fans
>Plastic fans
>Gauze mounted fans
>Fans with machine-made lace
>Fans with plain satin mounts
>Any fan which is badly damaged

Other fans come in the price range between these two categories and you pay what you can afford.

There are three ways in which to buy fans: privately, through a dealer and at auction sales. The first is done mainly by the very experienced collector, often at the end of an auction sale and especially if the fans have been sold as a lot. Beginners who buy privately are really asking for trouble, partly because they have no idea of prices and partly because they foolishly trust the owner for genuine details.

Buying through a dealer is a very good idea. Most dealers are well-known in the collecting world and they have a reputation to maintain. They allow you to handle a fan for some time and, should you buy, you know you have bought the fan which you handled and not another: i.e., you can handle during the preview of an auction, but so can others, and you may emerge with a fan that has been damaged after you saw it. Also the dealer gets to know your tastes, looks out on your behalf, or even buys in for you at auction so that others do not know the fan is really for you. Dealers are patient people who enjoy what they sell; I have heard several say, after attending an auction sale, 'Two for me and one for stock.' They know a very great deal on their subject but, at the same time, they do not expect the customer to 'pick their brains'. Their stock may be a trifle more expensive than fans at a sale, but they show a choice and it is *they* who have had to fight to get to a big sale, *they* who have had to take the risks and *they* who have had to spend their time and money in acquiring stock. Many dealers keep a small selection of 'cheapies' for beginners to buy to practise upon, and, naturally, they always have their customers in mind. It is sensible for beginners to work up a good relationship with some dealer for they will rarely be let down and, when the time comes (as it will) that the owner needs to sell an unwanted fan, then the dealer might take it in part-exchange or even arrange a sale.

The other side of the coin is the fun of a gamble in the auction sale. Beginners should go to the preview before the sale and immediately buy a catalogue. They should study this first, marking any lots which seem to appeal, and then go and look at their choice. Equally important is to study the 'estimated prices', a present-day advantage to all buyers which lends a good deal of spice to the proceedings.

In the past few years, in London, fans have emerged into a category of their own: no longer do they lurk among toys and costume, and

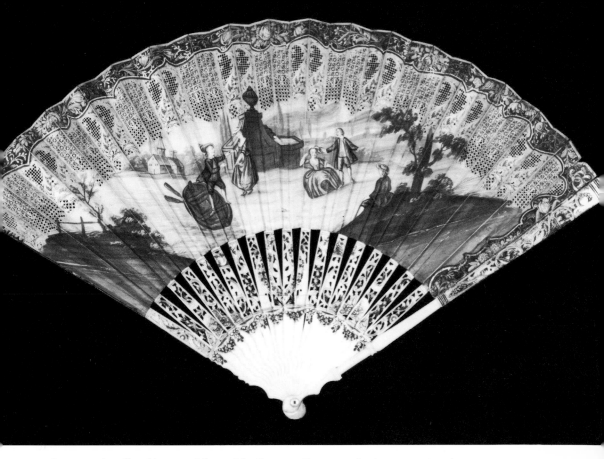

3. An eminently collectable painted decoupé fan depicting figures in a landscape, on pierced, carved and painted ivory sticks. c. 1770. $11\frac{1}{2}''$: 29.25 cms. By courtesy of Bonhams, Knightsbridge.

no longer are they sold in miserable lots, bundled up together, but as single items.

Catalogues are the fan buyers' bible. Most enthusiasts have the catalogue for each fan sale sent to them whether they intend to buy or not, and use it as reference material. Some people buy two catalogues, one to mark with comments—the price fetched and who bought it—and one to keep as an investment with any acquired fan. In this way the movement of prices can be seen, the new categories noted (i.e. advertising fans are now sold singly on occasion) and, occasionally, an 'old friend' may come up for sale a second time and the collector might pick up something that was missed before.

An 'estimated price' is just that. No auction house can guarantee what the day will bring: how tastes might suddenly change or if all the 'big' collectors have gone away on holiday at the same time. You can pick up a bargain if you are quick; you can lose something that you dearly want because you are intimidated, for the moment, by glares from the opposition; or you can find something that attracts you enormously that you missed at the preview.

To buy without having seen and examined a prospective purchase is sheer folly; but, once seen, to leave a bid with the sale room staff is an extremely good idea—they will not go mad on your behalf and you can rely on them.

Many 'big' collectors are tough, single-minded and ruthless. Once the catalogue of any sale has been studied you can learn to guess who will be present to buy the best. Watch who is at the viewing, or at the sale, and watch when the important people swiftly and silently leave the room. Many collectors are secretive for two main reasons: firstly for security and secondly because it is the very nature of the species. It is always wise not to enquire too closely what a collector has bought or has in his collection; it seems as impertinent as asking to look at his bank balance. Wait for an invitation!

Buying (or selling) through auction houses can be great fun and there is always the chance of a bargain. However, it is wise to examine with great care all the fine print, discover any hidden charges or premiums, and to remember that the auctioneers never take any risks themselves.

2 Historical Background

The use of the fan dates from the dawn of time as it accompanied the sun around the world, cooling people down. Today, in spite of the availability of air-conditioning units, fans are still being made, and used, in hot countries.

The earliest fan may have been a large leaf, or plaited straw in the same basic shape, with an added handle. At the same time fans were made from bunches of birds' feathers.

All over the world pretty feathers from rare birds have always been used for decorative purposes. One of man's earliest diversions was to tame or cage birds, to listen to their song and to admire their plumage. He would take a feather which attracted him and place it in his hair (some tribes still do, especially in Borneo) as a sign of comparative wealth, privilege or social standing. This use of a feather 'on high' is still retained today although few people really know the reason why. Feather shapes in diamonds (*aigrettes*) are worn by ladies in society, feathers curled around hats are worn by ambassadors, feathers in cere-monial head-dresses are worn all around the world, from crack Italian regiments to doormen outside first-class hotels—and feathers are even featured upon the heads of the magnificent Lipizzaner horses in Vienna.

The bird in the cage would beat his wings and provide a cool breeze, so what more natural than for the owner to pluck out a few brilliant feathers and make his very own 'bird's wing', the first real fan? In the sub-continent of India the Hindi generic term for a fan is *pankha*, from *pankh* meaning a feather or bird's wing. In China the archaic symbol for a fan looks like, and means, 'a bird's wing', and the newer word *shan* means 'feathers under a roof'. The same basically applies to Japan. Surely all of this is no mere coincidence?

There are three main shapes for fans: the fixed fan, the brisé fan and the folding fan.

THE FIXED FAN

This is rigid in shape and generally has a handle to hold. It can measure between six inches (15 cms) and two feet (60 cms) across, but is rarely larger. It can be shaped like a leaf, circular, like a spade or a flag, or sometimes indeterminate. I came across a beautiful one recently, painted upon a terracotta jar, *c* 380 BC, at the Museum in Benevento, near Naples (No. 372). The leaf was spade-shaped and dropped into a long wooden handle. The fixed fan has both advantages and disadvantages in its rigidity: the advantage being that it can be decorated on both sides in the most elaborate way; the disadvantage that if it is so decorated it cannot be put down on any surface but needs to be placed in a fan-holder. These holders seem common enough in the East but are never seen in the West.

An example is one of those delightful Chinese *pien-mien* which are

4. Pair of Handscreens, made of cream silk, double, stretched over strong wire frames and bound in blue silk, oversewn with twisted threads, formerly silver. Shaped handles. The central embroidery is in narrow ribbons, chenille, silk braids, silk threads, aerophane. Refs: Needlework Through the Ages by Symonds and Preece and Domestic Needlework by Seligman and Hughes. Third quarter of the 18th century. Total length 16½" : 42 cms. Total width 5½" : 14 cms. Owned by Mrs Pamela Hudson.

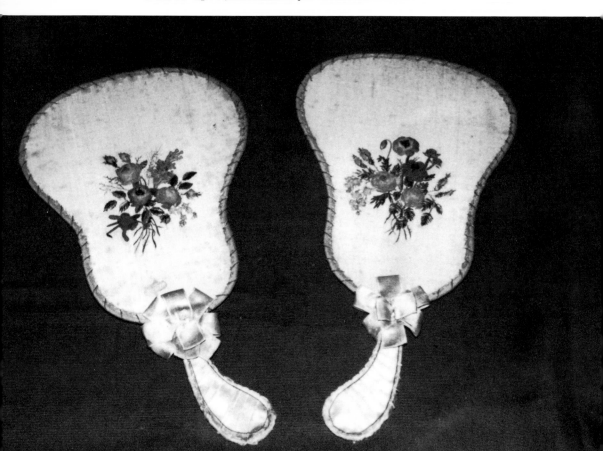

5. Ivory brisé fan, very rare, in the form of a double barrelled flintlock sporting gun, the sticks pierced, and the guardsticks silvered with the lock-plate, and carved to form the barrels, trigger and lock-plate. $11\frac{1}{2}$" : 29 cms. c 1780. (Fetched £1100 in August 1981.) By courtesy of Christies, South Kensington.

basically made from paper stretched over a wire frame, liberally coated and strengthened with glue, covered by pure gold-leaf and then elaborately decorated with a scene of birds and flowers made from tiny, iridescent kingfisher feathers held in gold wire. These flowers and birds can stand proud of their background by up to two inches (5 cms)— nothing will crush as the fan does not fold; it is carefully held in the hand by an applied handle, often of carved ivory.

THE BRISÉ FAN
Whether the brisé fan originated from China or from Japan is a matter of dispute. Its shape probably came from the use of writing tablets held in the hands of court officials. These were made from various materials, mainly wood or ivory, which were thin and light and easy to write the characters upon, from top to bottom. In order to keep them tidy and in order, a hole was made at the bottom of each and a cord used to tie them together. There appears to be certain evidence from paintings and carvings, and an example was found inside an image

22

6. *Chinese ivory brisé fan of a very high quality.* $7\frac{1}{2}''$: *19 cms. Made in Canton, c 1780. From* Fans of Imperial China, *by Neville Iröns, by courtesy of* The House of Fans Limited.

of Kannon (at the Toji temple at Kyoto), which shows that the slips or tablets might *just* have been the origin of the brisé fan, but there is no definite proof to be found anywhere.

Whatever its origin, the brisé fan as we know it takes the form of thin, light slips of ivory, wood, etc., which are held firmly together by a rivet or cord at the base and, along the top, initially by connecting threads, and later, by fine, thin connecting silk ribbons. This thread or ribbon is passed through or round the slips (or sticks) so cunningly that the brisé fan can fold up when not in use. On the whole this type of fan relies for its appeal upon the crafting of the material (carving, piercing, lacquering, etc.) or upon a painted scene. Any extraneous decoration (shibayama inlay, etc.) would only be placed upon the out-side of the guards.

Oriental brisé fans place far less emphasis upon the guardsticks than do European brisé fans; indeed, the earliest Japanese brisé fans made no attempt to distinguish the guards at all: the fans were made of many sticks, identical in length, breadth and thickness, and held together with either a metal rivet or a cord, with a decoration which spread right across all the sticks. Later, the end sticks were made thicker for protec-tion, and often decorated in a different manner from the sticks, and we now call these 'guards' because that was their function.

It appears that the earliest wooden sticks were wide (about one inch

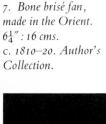

7. *Bone brisé fan, made in the Orient.* $6\frac{1}{4}''$: *16 cms. c. 1810–20. Author's Collection.*

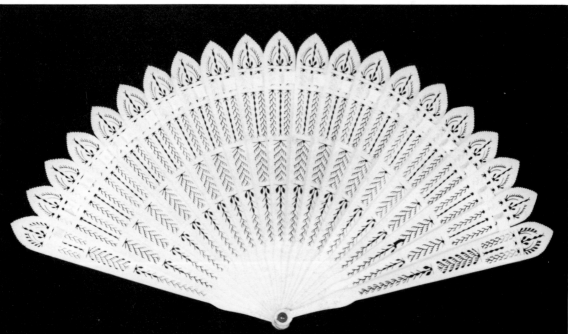

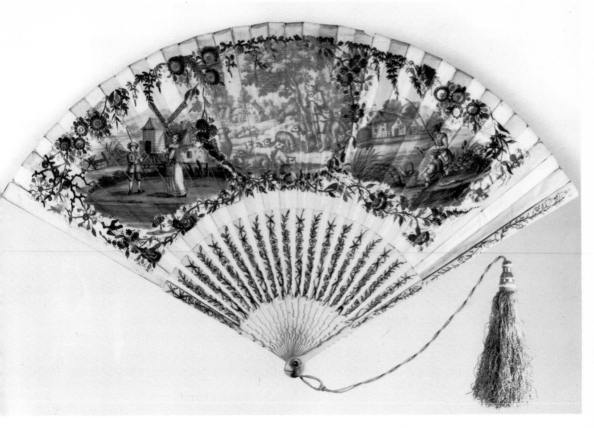

8. *English fan, the leaf with a central masked mezzotint printed in bistre probably by Bernard Lens, the reserves painted with two fishermen, and a farmer and his wife, within garlands of exotic flowers; the ivory sticks inlaid with tinted mother-of-pearl flowers. 10½″: 26.5 cms. c 1720. (Fetched £520 in July 1982.) By courtesy of Christies, South Kensington.*

or 2.5 cms) and the earliest pleats for folded fans took on the same width. In either case the need for a careful balance was paramount and explains why earlier, pre-seventeenth century brisé fans lacked heavy guards.

THE FOLDING FAN

The folding fan may have originated in either China or Japan: in view of the fact that so much Japanese art and culture stemmed from China, it seems probable that folding fans were a Chinese invention. No one knows for certain, and very few people care (except for a little pedantic in-fighting which goes on from time to time), but it seems generally agreed that the folding fan is Oriental in origin and that it emulates a bird's wing—many are referred to as 'bat fans'. In the past, relying heavily on the painstaking research of MacIver Percival and Wooliscroft Rhead, authors stated that the Japanese invented the folding fan and that the Chinese first had the idea of decorating it with a painted scene; recent equally painstaking research contradicts these statements, and only the dedicated scholar of the future will be able to provide proof one way or another. (For a description please see Chapter 3, 'Parts of a Fan'.)

There is a very early folding fan in existence in Europe. It is a cockade flabellum (a circular, pleated, folding fan which packs up into a box) or religious ceremonial fan, which was presented to the Basilica of St John the Baptist at Monza (near Milan) by the sixth century Queen Theodolinda of the Lombards.

There is no real start to the history of the fan; in each warm country in turn people have used them, and their decoration has altered in tune with all other decorative arts. In a way, the use of a fan to cool oneself has been as natural as the use of a drinking vessel to hold liquids—and no one has thought very much about either until their manufacture and decoration became refined.

We rely very much on early bas-reliefs, sculpture and painting in order to learn about contemporary fashions and customs. In this way we know of Egyptian fan-bearers, and proof has been provided in the handsome example discovered in the tomb of King Tutankhamun (c 1350 BC): a gold pole for a standard fan with a chased design upon it of the young god/king hunting ostriches—presumably for their fine white feathers.

Another historic example is the fan owned by Montezuma which can be seen today in the Museum für Völkerkunde in the Hofburg, Vienna. It was one of six pieces of the Montezuma Treasure sent over by Cortez to the Hapsburg King Charles V of Spain in 1524, then transferred to the Hapsburg Castle Ambras, and finally taken to the Hapsburg Palace in Vienna. It was more valuable than gold, for it was his symbol of authority. This example is a circular fixed fan, a mosaic of bright feathers applied to a wood and leather base and surrounded by an iridescent ruff of quetzal feathers; it was held on high on a bamboo pole.

Through writings, poems and excavations from tombs we also know of many ancient fans from the East. For example, in a burial mound of the sixth century AD in Fukuoka prefecture, on the island of Kyushu, are what are probably the earliest representations of fans in Japanese art; or again, in the Ma-wang-tui tomb site near Changsha in Hunan province were found two woven bamboo side-mounted fans of the second century BC, the earliest extant Chinese examples.

I am inclined to believe that fans were so universally used in warm areas that they were not dramatically introduced into Europe in the sixteenth century at all (as some previously believed) but, through the newly developing trade routes, new types of fans came through from the Orient to add to those already here. These new styles excited the interest of the ladies of the courts of Europe and they were pounced upon, used, and proudly displayed. Their display coincided with the new fashion of having portraits painted of people other than royalty, so the wealthy merchants and their wives were portrayed sporting the latest fashions in dress, and ladies' fans were seen at last, together with the newest accessories, such as gloves and handkerchiefs.

The history of the fan in both China and Japan is voluminous, and one can only suggest that the new collector slowly and steadily devours all the books listed in the Bibliography. In Chapter 3 some of their many types are explained, but it is only fair to stipulate that writers of the Orient always consider fans as a vehicle for various stages of

9. Rare Oriental fan, possibly made for export. The leaf is of paper, symmetrically cut out for mica panels to be inserted (now missing) and, in between, there are painted panels with mother-of-pearl chips. There are painted ivory sticks and pierced and painted guards, terminating in a reversed tulip-shaped finial and having a domed metal pivot. Late 17th century. Private Collection.

painting, etc., in their very long art history—that is, when they are discussing fans which were painted for their home market. 'Export' fans are a different matter. The artists and craftsmen of both China and Japan are extremely well documented; happily for us, many artists signed their names on any fan they considered worthy, often applying a date mark as well. If a collector has access to Chinese or Japanese libraries, and to scholars, then the task of identification and dating is much easier than with European fans.

In Europe the matter is considerably more difficult. As with all art history, the trained eye will be able to date a fan and even, on occasion, accurately suggest its country of origin. However there remains the question of whether a fan was made throughout by one person, or is a composite of styles and craftsmen. Mrs Pamela Hudson of Cirencester, England, once showed me a fan with French, Flemish, Persian and Chinese influences 'all thrown together with abandon' most successfully. Many people associate fans only with the French, or only with the Spanish, yet a hurried glance through any recent sales catalogue will show that they were made in Russia, Germany, Austria, the Netherlands, Italy and England, too. Some countries had Guilds (see Chapter 6), which helps identification; other areas, such as Germany or Italy, were not as we know them today but still divided into States, so that one should rather consider the arts of a city, such as Venice or Berlin.

Fans are not evaluated merely as an accessory to dress, although the less worthy ones can be directly tied to fashion, but in many cases they form part of European art history. They also reflect the best of the miniature crafts, especially those in which weight is no consideration. One must also bear in mind that the fans of the sixteenth, seventeenth and eighteenth centuries were generally extremely expensive and that the prices they fetch today may still be relatively cheap. European and American fans of the nineteenth century eventually became astonishingly cheap (some were sold for one farthing) when they were machine-made or imported by the thousand from the East. The prices fetched for a fan ten years ago were five hundred per cent cheaper than today, but I believe that a clever collector can still build up a splendid collection and, in a few years' time, find that all the hard-won expertise has been more than worthwhile; aesthetically, a whole new world will have opened up, and dozens of new friends will have been acquired along the way.

3 Catalogue: Fan Types, Styles, Materials

The Bibliography at the end of this book gives a comprehensive list of books about fans, and therefore I do not propose to cover these well-worn paths again. Unfortunately almost all the books are now out of print, but they can often be bought in specialist shops dealing with costume subjects or art; it is always worth writing to any of the following:

> *Lesley Hodges*, Costume & Fashion Bookshop,
> Queen's Elm Parade, Old Church Street,
> London SW3 6EJ.
> *Daphne Lucas*,
> 28 Addison Way, London NW11 6AP.
> *K. E. Skafte*,
> DK-4800 Nykobing 3/Falster. Denmark.

Many of the books mentioned can be found in libraries and all of them are available in National Libraries such as the British Museum.

The following catalogue is an attempt to standardise terms used in the fan world and especially to help those who wish to buy at auction.

ADHESIVES
In the past most forms of adhesive were secret formulae which were jealously guarded by different manufacturers. They have already been adequately covered in previous books on fans (see Bibliography).

ADVERTISING FANS
On the whole these were made, not for sale to the public, but to be given away as advertising gimmicks for various hotels, drinks, soap, etc., in the way that plastic or paper carrier bags are today.

They were pretty, cheap gifts with a good deal of public relations impact, rather in advance of contemporary advertising in newspapers

KISHINCHAND CHELLARAM
NEAR D'ANGLIS No. 181 MOUNTROAD
MADRAS
MANUFACTURER OF
MADRAS FANCY EMBROIDERY & SILVER WARE
DEALERS IN
INDIAN, CHINESE JAPANESE SILKS & CURIOS

10. Advertising fan, made in Japan and printed in India. The paper leaf is printed in colours; the sticks are of wood. Early 20th century. 8½″: 21.75 cms. Owned by Mrs Margaret Little.

or journals. They may have been 'give-aways' but they were not 'throw-aways', for those were the days when people were loyal to a shop or hotel, and if they had been given a fan freely they felt that they then had a moral obligation to look after it and continue to patronise that establishment.

They come in every size and shape, smaller fans being more usual. Few were made before 1850 and the majority come from the first quarter of the twentieth century. So far, it is known that one group of collectors has unearthed over 1,500 different types, picking them up casually on bric-a-brac stalls. I know of three similar fans advertising an hotel: in 1970 one was bought for five pence, in 1975 another changed hands for £5 and in 1981 a third was for sale for £85—an indication of the general rise in the value of a fan.

Over 50% of advertising fans started life in Japan with cheap, unadorned wooden or bamboo sticks and a plain or floral leaf made of paper, fabric, chicken skin or even cardboard. Imported by the thousand into Europe or the United States, they were then overprinted by the advertising company with its slogan or decoration; others were merely stamped along the guardstick. It is very easy to find identical advertising fans with merely the names of different firms printed or stamped on them. Most other advertising fans are of a better quality and much more personal.

Collectors are now beginning to specialise: some buy only silk fans, other buy those which have a sample of the goods they advertise (such as Piver scent, etc.), others concentrate on French advertising fans, and so on. Up until now all advertising fans have been lumped into one category, but I believe that shortly they will be categorised in sales; they are a fascinating category for new collectors, with all the separate branches, and a great many can still be had for very small sums. See also COMMEMORATIVE FANS.
Illustration Nos. X, 10.

AIDE MEMOIRE FANS
Towards the end of the eighteenth century there appeared many fans which were designed to jog the memory: printed with dance steps, words and music of a contemporary song, historical data, rules for card-games and a variety of other information. For some there were plans of theatres and their numbered boxes, for others there were details of botanical specimens and flowers newly popularised by the travels of Captain Cook and Sir Joseph Banks. The majority were made during the latter half of the eighteenth century and into the first quarter of the nineteenth. Although they were generally printed, some were then hand-coloured, and often they were mounted on to cheap wooden sticks. The materials used for the leaf were as varied as those for advertising fans. Today they are quite rare.

ALMANAC FANS
During the eighteenth century there were some printed fans, often made of paper, which displayed an annual calender, several incorporating varous events as well; they were meant to be thrown away at the end of the year. In the nineteenth century the makers became far more inventive in their designs and other materials were used, from cardboard to silk and satin. See illustration in *The Book of Fans,* page 26.

APPLIED FACES FANS

These fans were made in China, strictly for the export trade, being highly coloured and having an enormous popularity in Europe, during the nineteenth century. They are normal folding fans with a paper leaf painted with a scene showing Chinese men and women. The figures sometimes have silken robes applied to them and (and this is the main novelty) the faces of the people are of painted, shaped pieces of ivory. They cannot, by the greatest stretch of the imagination, be called 'art'; they are pure exercises in craft, which is both why the Victorians enjoyed them so much and why they were not used by the Chinese themselves. It is also the reason for calling them not 'mandarin fans' (which would be a sarcastic insult), but 'applied faces' fans.

The practice of painting scenes thronged with people, often to commemorate some occasion, is well-known in China; moreover, during the Ch'ien Lung period (1736–1795) there was a vogue for bone and feather pictures which led to fans also being made with applications of mica, straw, feathers and silk. During the same period, similar fans were being made in Europe, but in a different style, with slightly larger applications of ivory for the painted faces, and including a neck as well as a face (several c 1760 are extant). European fans of this period and type are also known, with painted faces made from a soft chamois leather; by their style they seem to be made in France. The European

11. Applied Faces fan, the leaf mounted on ornately enamelled, pierced and carved gilt metal sticks. Probably Canton. c 1850. 11″ : 28 cms. By courtesy of Bonhams, Knightsbridge.

I. Telescopic, Applied Faces fan opened to its fullest extent. The leaf is covered with ivory applied faces, and applied silk robes; the sticks are of black and gold lacquer on wood; the double silk tassel hangs from a loop. Made in Macao. 9″: 23 cms. Mid-19th century. Private Collection.

II. The same fan displayed when 'shut down'.

III. Detail of the reverse showing a central scene, in a cartouche (one of three) of the Port at Macao. This fan could also loosely come under the category of a 'Topographical' fan.

IV. Lace fan. The leaf is of very fine Brussels mixed lace, brilliantly embroidered overall with diamanté which flashes fire as it is fluttered. The sticks are of mother-of-pearl. 14″: 35.5 cms. c 1880. Private Collection.

V. Detail of the lace fan, showing the superb crafting of the mother-of-pearl sticks and guards, with a 'goldfish' backing and tonal gilding.

versions then had ivory or bone sticks and guards crafted in the chinoiserie style, whereas those made in China were made from a multitude of materials: carved, pierced or lacquered woods, ivory, bone, mother-of-pearl and metal filigree.

The Applied Faces fans of China can be vaguely dated by the number of figures they include—the earliest having the fewest, the latest having a great many—which led to some being named 'fans of one thousand faces', although it is rare to see more than 50 on each side. These fans came from two distinct places, Canton and Macao. Neville Iröns has done some important work on identifying both makers and artists (especially in Macao) and it is worth reading his book *Fans of Imperial China*. One type, from Canton, generally had the figures on both sides and was relatively quieter in colouring, being made 'for the rest of Europe': the other type came from Macao and was much brighter, often with a silvered or gilded paper on the reverse painted with long-tailed birds and large flowers, or sometimes with views of harbours in vignettes; these were destined for Spain or Portugal. In every case these fans give an appearance of being rich, innovative and individual, and they repay hours of study under a magnifying glass to delight the owner; they were made for about 100 years. See also MANDARIN FANS. Illustration Nos. I, 11, 34.

ARTICULATED FANS

These were made in Europe between 1760 and 1830 and were a speciality of the Germans. In appearance perfectly normal folding fans for their country or period, they also have well-carved and crafted sticks and guards. On the upper section of the guardstick there is featured some small scene, often under a protective material such as glass or an Essex crystal, in the shape of an elongated oval: many of these tiny scenes have no decorative connection with that of the leaf. Alongside this scene on the guard, hidden among the general crafting, is a tiny metal rod, and when the rod is either pushed up or pulled down, something in that scene alters; for example, one known scene shows a 'lady of quality' with a tiny mask in her hand: when the rod is moved a hinge at her elbow permits her to raise the mask to cover her eyes. Another shows a gentleman out shooting and when he raises his gun a gamebird drops to his feet; another shows a woman chopping vegetables in a kitchen.

It seems possible that these articulated scenes were made by toy-makers or jewellers, but because of their delicacy they obviously had a short life. There are, however, two types of articulated fan: firstly the earlier ones which are complicated and mechanical with hidden hinged rods activating the movement, and secondly those which tailed off into a more simplified manual movement with no hidden rods, as seen in children's books.

Illustration No. XXXIX.

ASSIGNAT FANS

A British £1 note has the words, 'I promise to pay the Bearer the sum of . . .' and an Assignat fan is a skit on these words (literally: to assign to) dating from the time of the French Revolution, when the French monetary system was in chaos. Many people paid their accounts with IOUs (assignats) and some contemporary fans were made with a scattering of these useless promissory notes on the leaf. Sometimes the design incorporated a playing card showing the seven of diamonds. These printed (occasionally hand-coloured) paper Assignat fans were made between 1789 and 1797; when the monetary system stabilised the fans were no longer made and were either thrown away or stored. They are rather rare, but there is a good collection of them in the Museum in Geneva—understandable with the Swiss interest in Banking.

See illustration in *The Fan*, page 82.

ASYMMETRICAL FANS

The Oriental world was very aware of the fact that the Japanese relished a joke, enjoyed a novelty and were not averse to an object being made with an asymmetrical design. The Chinese, on the other hand, preferred symmetry but, towards the middle of the nineteenth century, they seem to have made some fine fans in an asymmetrical shape for export to Japan, together with asymmetrically shaped porcelain objects. In turn, when released to trade worldwide, the Japanese copied these fans and exported them to France. They are large, generally with either a black or a red background, made of fine linen applied to thick or thin paper, silk or satin, and then decorated with bold designs of flowers, birds, or figures, many in black and white and a good deal of gold. The sticks too are large and made of gold and black lacquer on fine wood. When folded, the fans' sticks give a 'stepped' appearance.

According to *The Lady's World* of 1887, a taste for asymmetry emerged and 'skirts now never have two sides alike'; the Japanese export in folding fans with an asymmetrical shape dates to this period.

AUTOGRAPH FANS

These are almost always of the nineteenth or the early twentieth century. They are either wooden brisé fans of some considerable size, or folding, made of stout paper, because in each case they were designed to be autographed by people unused to 'decorating' a fan. Some merely have signatures upon them, others have sketches or paintings. One of the most famous is the Messel Autograph Fan, one of a collection in private hands, a large wooden brisé fan, now displayed in a splendid case with glass on both sides in order to show the wealth of autographed sketches and paintings made by friends of Linley Sambourne. He was an artist who contributed to *Punch* in the late nineteenth century; the friends included some of the most distinguished artists of the period and it is possible that the fan was decorated in Linley Sambourne's house in Stafford Terrace in London (now open to the public).

These fans also come under the category 'commemorative fans': nothing is more frustrating, however, than to find an autographed fan with absolutely no reference to the event it commemorates.

BALLOONING FANS

Because of its rarity this type of commemorative fan now has a category of its own. It first appeared as part of the widespread enthusiasm for ballooning in the eighteenth century, although there exist pastiches (copies) made in the nineteenth century. The Montgolfier brothers (Joseph and Etienne) invented the first hot air balloon and got it off the ground in Southern France on 5th June, 1783. As a result, some of the earliest fans are also known as 'Montgolfières'. Other inventors created hot air balloons and hydrogen balloons (Blanchard and Professor Charles) soon afterwards. All the fans are hand-coloured, some displaying a flurry of national flags, and all, naturally, have to show the balloon upon them, too. They had a very short life.

BAMBOO

Most Oriental fans are catalogued thus: 'sticks: bamboo', and the collector passes on, unthinking. Yet the bamboo is an extraordinarily 'elegant grass' which occurs naturally in every continent except Europe and Antarctica, but seems happiest in southern Asia. In the world there are about one thousand species of bamboo, of some 50 genera. In Japan there are 662 species, from 13 genera; in China 300 species, of 26 genera. The most striking characteristic of bamboo is its growth—no other living thing grows so tall so fast. Near Kyoto a Japanese scientist measured the world's record: a culm (woody stalk) of *ma-dake* (*Phyllostrachys bambusoides*), Japan's commonest bamboo, grew almost four feet in 24 hours. The Chinese were the first to appreciate the beauty and usefulness of bamboo; their ancient dictionary, the *Erh Ya*, written 1000 years before Christ, referred to it and it is also known to have been both split and glued at that time.

Long before the invention of paper in the second century BC, China's earliest records were written on slips of green bamboo. It is easy to scratch or incise on bamboo's smooth skin, a quality unique in the plant kingdom. To make a bamboo book, strips were strung together with silk or ox sinew—one such bundle of 312 slips was recently unearthed in a Han Dynasty (second century BC) tomb.

Apart from bamboo's practical uses, in the Orient it is considered very beautiful. In China they call bamboo the chief member of the trio of 'Winter friends'—bamboo, Winter plum and pine—and the three occur throughout Chinese art and literature as symbols of resistance to hardship. The plum flowers while snow is still on the ground, the pine flourishes in poor soil and clings to precipitous cliffs, and the bamboo remains green throughout the year.

Bamboo, for many purposes, is lighter and stronger than steel. One of the engineering marvels of the world is the great bridge over the Min River in Sichuan (still in use after more than 1000 years) hanging from bamboo cables nearly seven inches in diameter, wound round capstans so that they can be tightened like tuning a guitar.

Bamboo is said to have a peculiarity: most species flower only at long intervals—30, 60 or even 120 years apart—and then they die. At about the same time, all plants of the same species—wherever they are in the world—will burst into flower. When this happens the culms die, the fallen seeds take root, but it may be from five to ten years before a bamboo seedling reaches full maturity and growth.

In India, it is said, bamboo is the poor man's multipurpose timber and he literally lives with it from birth to death. One-fifth of India's forest reserves are bamboo, from which the people cut selectively. In Japan most of the bamboo flourishes in the mild climate of Kyushu, the southernmost island, although the bamboo capital is Kyoto. The Japanese use bamboo for decoration and the decorative arts far more than do the Chinese; the variety of objects extends from flutes and furniture, via torture instruments, to the comfort of the 'bamboo wife'—a woven basketwork cylinder about five feet long, which the sleeper embraces (on very hot nights) and throws one leg over, so that cooling breezes can pass through.

Bamboo used for fan sticks is often from the 'tea stick' variety, named for its colour resembling freshly brewed tea. It has to be three to five years old before cutting because new culms are mostly water and if you cut them they will shrink and crack as they dry. Once cut they are cleaned with fine sand, then left in the sun for ten days. Afterwards they are straightened over a fire and then cut to length.

The use of bamboo for sticks is not to be lightly passed over, nor is it easy to pin-point which of the thousand species is being used. 'Green-striped', 'Black' (from China), 'Mottled' (from Sri Lanka), 'Golden', 'Giant' (from Burma), 'Square' and 'Tortoiseshell' are but seven different species.

It is noticeable, too, that the guards are very often of a different variety of bamboo from the sticks, often painted to match their colour, the sticks remaining as Nature made them. This is because of the length between 'nodes' or joints of the bamboo: as the guardstick had to be wider or thicker or longer, it often came from a different plant and was then disguised by paint or lacquer.

Since bamboo has a parallel grain, sticks can be evenly and cleanly cut to size and then polished. Bamboo sticks can also remain attached to the culm, leaving it as a handle, when making 'uchiwa' fans. Charlotte Salwey gave this description in her book *Fans of Japan*, published in 1894:

> About eighteen inches of bamboo is cut and prepared, of which about nine inches is split down to the node or joint which prevents further splitting. As the grain runs perfectly straight, fifty or sixty segments are obtained by careful division of exactly the same thickness. In order to keep these in position, a diminutive bow

of thick bamboo is inserted just below the joint, the segments are deftly arranged crossways, and a string having two strands is interlaced alternately between them and fastened securely: by this tension the whole framework is steadied. Though the handle is generally formed by the few inches of bamboo left below the node, other substitutes are sometimes employed for the handles, which are left either plain or embellished: coloured and naturally curved bamboo, notched and carved in an open manner, is frequently resorted to for a change. When this is the case a circular piece of thick paper or thin wood is doubled so that the lower portion of the fan is dropped into a slot and fixed with a small brass nail or rivet; but the framework of this fan is always constructed on the plan previously entered upon.

The Japanese have a reverence for natural beauty so, on the whole, they did not embellish their bamboo sticks and guards. When they did so the decoration was lightly painted in a contrasting but self-colour and the better examples were different on each side of the sticks. However, they also have a keen competitive spirit and when they made fans for the export market they sometimes inlaid the guards with ivory, wood or metals. This attitude appears similar to the change from making fans with a single leaf (which is normal for Japan) to a double leaf (more normal for China) when considering the export trade. Illustration Nos. VII, XXXII, XXXIII.

BAROQUE
This term, derived from the Portuguese word *barroco* (Spanish *barrueco*) meaning a rough or imperfect pearl, was originally used in a pejorative sense to describe seventeenth century Italian art and that of the other countries, particularly Germany, which were under Italian influence. In the decorative arts, Baroque was distinguished by a return to classical forms, but used in a totally unclassical way. Its vogue lasted from *c* 1600 to *c* 1715, when the Rococo began to take over. The earlier period was dovetailed with the High Renaissance and the latter for many years with the Rococo. It is a style of movement and freedom: in architecture buildings were designed to evoke emotional responses from those who entered them; the use of light and shade was treated in a totally different way, perspectives were adjusted, grandeur and magnificence were seen

12. Italian baroque fan, the vellum leaf painted with Mary visiting Elizabeth, meeting on the steps before a house, surrounded by other figures and putti in a rural setting; the reverse decorated with painted flowers: mounted on carved ivory sticks inlaid with mother-of-pearl and piqué point. In free-standing glazed case, fan shaped. Early 18th century. 10″: 25.5 cms. By courtesy of Bonhams, Knightsbridge.

from canvases to ceilings, colours were heavy and often dark in tone; 'all the world was a stage' and there was a great interest in classical mythology.

All of this can be seen interpreted on fans from *c* 1650 to *c* 1730, especially those made in France, England and the Netherlands. Many baroque fans had a spread of 18 inches (45 cms), with sticks of tortoise-shell or ivory which bore absolutely no reference to each other in their design and often appeared as a stark contrast. The leaf was dark in tone, whether of parchment or rag-paper; the painted scene continued right across from one side to the other without any breaks for vignettes, etc., and the subject matter was very grand, sometimes being surrounded by a scattering of flowers and leaves outlined with gold.

These fans usually reach a high price in sales, especially if undamaged in any way; some have been removed from their sticks and mounted as paintings. It should be noted that they really *were* easel paintings, cut to a fan-shape and applied to sticks. There is very rarely any indication that the painter wished to follow the shape of the fan in his composition, unlike the Orientals, who always considered the shape. Illustration No. 12.

BATTOIR FANS

This type applies to normal folding fans which had very few, large and curiously shaped sticks called 'battoirs' because they looked like flat guitars, or bats, or racquets for 'bat and ball'. The leaf was usually highly decorated in order to balance the bold design of the sticks—sometimes as few as six or eight in number—which were pierced, carved and generally highly crafted (sometimes interspersed with very plain, straight sticks for practical purposes); the guard-stick did not necessarily have the same shaping but did have similar crafting. Because there were so few sticks, this led to very wide pleats in the leaf and there were endless attempts to balance sticks and leaf in weight.

Most battoir fans are labelled 'Spanish' although, as a very loose rule, those made in the eighteenth century with ivory or bone sticks and guards were actually made in France for export to Spain; it was those made in the nineteenth century of plain or painted woods that originated in Spain for the home market.

BONBORI FANS

The first Japanese fans had only a single leaf, whereas Chinese fans originally had double leaves (and they still like to work this way although there are obvious exceptions). During the Muromachi period (1392–1568) Chinese double fans were introduced into Japan and, to deal with the increased thickness of the leaf, two new types of fan were developed. One type was the bonbori, with guardsticks which bent inwards at the wider end, holding the thicker leaf together (sometimes in what seemed a vicelike grip); the other type was the suehiro (q.v.).

BONE (See IVORY)

BRAZILIAN FANS
During the nineteenth century, a most prolific firm in Rio de Janeiro
(M. Luiza Bittacourt) used to make a frou-frou of a fixed fan. These
came in cardboard boxes of circular shape, with a handle, about six
inches deep, and a well-fitting lid—exactly like a hatbox. The fan was
made up of feathers, layer upon layer, upon a canvas support, often
with a tiny hummingbird alight in the centre. The colours were of
every shade of the rainbow, starting with white or tinted ducks'
feathers, the points of their quills to the centre, frothed over by maribou
and finally decorated by an iridescent hummingbird, or tiny iridescent
beetles, or both. The other side of the fan was kept flat (so that it could
be laid to rest) and it was held by a handle of bone, wood or turned
ivory. In some cases the fans are made with feathers on both sides,
and in others, instead of the hummingbird, there are small, beautifully
made silk and feather flowers which come together with a flower
wreath—showing that these were made for either a bride or a debu-
tante. The fact that they were exported so often by this company leads
us to call them all 'Brazilian Fans', although other firms made them,
too. There is an interesting selection in the Museum in Bournemouth.
See illustration in *The Book of Fans*, page 90.

BRIDAL FANS (See MARRIAGE FANS)

BROKEN FANS (See TRICK FANS)

CABRIOLET FANS
I have been guilty in the past of misunderstanding the real reason be-
hind the shape of the cabriolet fan; I am especially grateful to Neville
Iröns for propelling me towards Peter Mann at the Science Museum,
London, for the latter's patient explanations and for information in
two books which have helped me: *Carriage Terminology: an Historical
Dictionary* by Don. H. Berkebile, Smithsonian Institution, Washington
1978 (page 64) and *Looking at Carriages* by Sallie Walrond, Pelham,
London 1980 (page 96).
   The cabriolet was introduced into Paris in 1755 by Josiah Childs
(who also designed it). A small, light-weight one-horse chaise which

could easily be driven by a daring lady driver, it had wheels of a very large diameter. The cabriolet had a curious motion when travelling because of its pair of long, springing shafts which made it buck and prance like a goat—its name came from the French *cabrioler*, to leap or to caper, because it was so light and frisky. The shape was like an elongated comma, or nautilus shell, which was most uncommon at that time. The third curious characteristic of the cabriolet was its hood: in order to leave room for the Tiger (or groom) to travel standing on a platform at the rear of the carriage, it was generally kept half-open when driving by means of a metal bar which radiated across the central section of the ribs of the hood . . . a new technique adapted later for the hoods of baby carriages.

Childs' cabriolet was the first of its type—in fact it did not become common in England until about 1794. Letters flew back and forth between Paris and the other capitals of fashion (especially London), and descriptions are extant of cabriolets being painted onto the garments of both sexes, just as we might buy a passing vogue today. Fans were immediately made to look something like the cabriolets, with the vehicle painted onto them, too.

The cabriolet fan is therefore distinguished by certain features: long, thin sticks like the shafts, an ordinary fan leaf but with the addition of a secondary one, like the strengthening bar across the ribs of the hood, placed across the centre of the sticks and, with the genuine ones *c* 1755–60, a painting of a lady driver with the hood of her cabriolet 'half-up'.

It now seems fairly safe to assume that all genuine cabriolet fans of the eighteenth century were made in France, that they should all have two leaves, that they should have thin, straight sticks and lastly, but by no means least, that they should have painted on them a scene of the driver and her 'cab'. Nineteenth century cabriolet fans are copies and show a variety of other small scenes. The double leaf has been seen on earlier fans (I know of two *c* 1740) so the painting of the vehicle is essential. There is also a ravishingly pretty treble-leafed fan in the Oldham Collection, Museum of Fine Arts, Boston.

CAMIEU FANS
This fan has a painting on the leaf of different tones and shades of the same basic colour, such as rose or blue or green. Shades of grey are

better known as 'grisaille' and used for mourning fans.

CANTON FANS (See APPLIED FACES FANS)

CARTOGRAPHIC FANS
These are rare today although they must have been a popular novelty
in their time, and they were made all over the world. Mostly made
of paper, although silk examples are known, they are generally printed
fans on cheap sticks, designed as a guide for the traveller, showing countries, counties or towns, and having been of help on a journey they
were then thrown away. Fans known are enormously varied: a map
of Switzerland (giving details of how many miles it was from Berne
to London or Rome, etc.), another showing the centre of Pekin, an
eighteenth century one showing the City of London, others showing
counties in England and a rare one on silk showing a map of Gibraltar.
See illustration in *Fans of Imperial China*, page 144.

CARTOUCHE
This is a term used to describe certain decoration upon a fan. A cartouche is ornamentation in a scroll form, applied especially to an elaborate framing around a design; by extension the word is applied to
any oval shape, or even to a decorative shield, whether scrolled or not.
A cartouche then refers to a decoration on a fan which has a scrolled
border or framing, isolating that decoration from the remainder of
the fan leaf. It can be a painting upon paper, vellum, etc., or embroidery

*13. The leaf of this fan
is painted with various
scenes in four curiously
shaped vignettes: the
ivory sticks carved,
pierced, painted and
gilt with figures and
scrolling and with
encrustations of carved
mother-of-pearl.
Probably Flemish.
11″: 28 cms. c 1750.
(Fetched £520 in
May 1982.) By
courtesy of Christies,
South Kensington.*

14. French fan, the leaf painted with five vignettes of different shapes, the reserves painted with fruit, flowers and lace with a peacock blue border; the ivory sticks carved and pierced in gilt with dancing figures and musicians, one guardstick set with a mother-of-pearl plaque inscribed with the initials J.J.P.B., the other guardstick set with a mother-of-pearl skull and carved with an ivory pierrot. 11″ : 28 cms. c 1765. (Fetched £300 March 1982.) By courtesy of Christies, South Kensington.

upon a textile, or carving upon brisé fans made from ivory or woods.

A *medallion* is similar to a cartouche, but the framing is either oval or circular and of a dominant size within the area of the leaf. A *reserve* is the smaller oval or shield-shape around a monogram on ivory or woods or around small scenes upon either leaf or sticks. It is possible for a cartouche, a medallion or a reserve to be centrally placed; it is also possible to have several upon a leaf or sticks.

A *vignette* is an overall term for a cartouche.
Illustration Nos. 13, 14.

CELLULOID FANS (See PLASTIC FANS)

CHAPEL FANS
Fans were made for use in churches years before worshippers in chapels decided to have their own version. The church fans (q.v.) are more

elaborate and overtly concerned for the Royal Family; chapel fans do not mention them. The first printed, stipple-engraved, uncoloured chapel fan was dated 1st May, 1796, and is entitled 'New Church Fan Published with the Approbation of the Lord Bishop of London' by the Rev. W. Peters. Chapel fans are usually of paper, but vellum was also used.

CHICKEN SKIN

This is an extremely fine type of parchment which was used for fan leaves. It 'snaps' like paper, is far more refined than the normal soft vellum used for fans in northern European countries and it has no grain. The finest type came from Persia and was used for tracing documents and miniatures, and was also used in the Mughal Courts. It is the skin taken from an unborn kid (killing the mother before its birth) and then prepared as a surface for painting. The earliest reached Europe via Venice, through trade with the Middle East and Levantine countries, and its use for fan leaves spread up through Europe during the

15. An 18th century painted fan, the chicken-skin leaf decorated with Diana and her attendants, mounted on finely worked silvered, gilded and jewelled mother-of-pearl sticks and guards. Possibly Dutch. 10½″ : 26.5 cms. By courtesy of Bonhams, Knightsbridge.

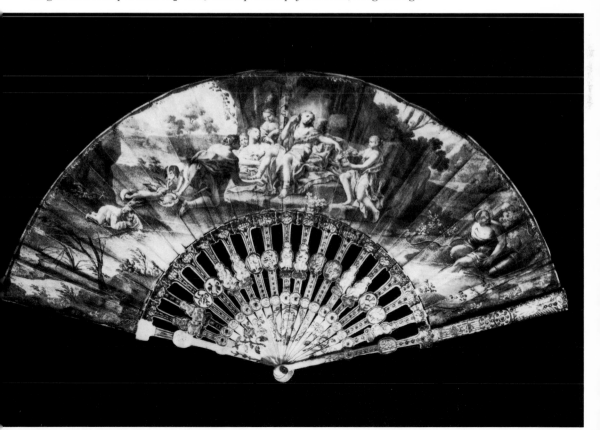

eighteenth century. Many of the finest fans are made with 'chicken-skin' leaves; the name stems from the similarity to the chicken's egg embryo skin, which is equally fine, light, strong and almost transparent when held up to the light. When used for fans sometimes more than one skin is glued together to make it more opaque. See also PARCHMENT. Illustration Nos. 15, 29, 35.

CHILDREN'S FANS

During the eighteenth century children were often treated merely as small adults in society, and therefore wore much the same fashions as their parents, but in a small size. This also applied to fans. Many tiny fans were as beautifully decorated for children as for their parents; some were educational but most were just smaller adult fans. They are much in demand today.

CHINESE IVORY BRISÉ FANS

These were made in China from the mid-seventeenth century as export fans to the West. The first type were small, wedge-shaped, made with

16. Chinese ivory brisé fan, of the transitional period when they began to be carved (for the first time) on both sides. Made in Canton. $7\frac{1}{2}''$: 19 cms. c 1800. From Fans of Imperial China, *by Neville Iröns, by courtesy of The House of Fans Limited.*

absolutely plain ivory sticks, and painted. Some of the painted scenes show European traders (Dutch or Portuguese) and occasionally there is a small amount of piercing through the ivory. Most of them came into Europe via Holland and were a great novelty. From these stem the 'Vernis Martin' fans (q.v.).

Between 1700–1720 a slightly different type of ivory brisé fan emerged. Again it was wedge-shaped, the ivory pierced in the upper half with a light, geometrical design (or with circular 'cash' shapes) in which certain sections were left solid. These formed 'canvases' for a painted scene, with gilding. The sticks were held by a fine, strong thread (not a ribbon which was not seen until about 1750), the rivet was metal and the guardsticks remained solid and unpierced until *c* 1740.

One point of recognition between Chinese ivory brisé fans and copies made in Europe is that the Europeans always placed their ribbon along the edge of the sticks and the Chinese invariably placed theirs in proper slots well below the edge of the sticks. Until *c* 1830 they also made a feature of the ribbon area, as if there was an implied border. From *c* 1710 the ivory on these fans was pierced through, but after *c* 1760 it was 'ribbed', showing fine, vertical parallel lines as a background, interspersed with small areas of carved ivory in the shape of flowers, leaves, birds, circles and shield-shapes. Small painted scenes were used as decorative motifs on ivory brisé fans from *c* 1710 until *c* 1750, when they finally disappeared, leaving the ivory creamy white, with a matching silk ribbon.

In size these fans were larger, finer and more supple during the eighteenth century and became shorter, cruder and thicker during the nineteenth. Some fans show a central shield shape, developed from earlier vignettes, in solid ivory: these were first painted and then developed into an area where the shape remained, the background was ribbed and a monogram was placed in the centre—carved to order in Europe. By *c* 1750 each individual stick suddenly acquired a rounded tip, and, in the main, the finest ivory brisé fans continued to have this form until well into the nineteenth century.

During the final quarter of the eighteenth century these fans seemed to divide into three separate parts: the area above the ribbon, the area below the ribbon and the area from the gorge to the rivet. Little decorative borders appeared surrounding each area, very fine and delicate, the main decoration within each border being totally different from the others, i.e.—the section above the ribbon could be circular, the central section could have a scattering of small flowers and leaves with ribbing and finely carved vignettes and the gorge section could be both solid and carved with elliptical shapes. At the turn of the century the section above the ribbon ceased to have identical designs on all sticks (usually flowers and leaves) and began to feature different scenes on each, such as those from Chinese life, Taoist or Buddhist symbols, etc.

To coincide with the new European fashions in dress at this time, fans became far smaller, some regaining their wedge-shape and losing their 'finger-tip' outline. The ribbed background persisted, and while above the ribbon the tiny scenes were all different, below it the overall design became fussier, more formalised, with more solid sections of carving showing scenes now of figures (a few to start with, many later on) and some architectural scenes.

Guardsticks throughout the eighteenth century generally appeared 'by a different hand'. From c 1710–1740 they were solid, with occasional touches of paint or gilding; from c 1740–c 1800 they were very often of exactly the same pattern, not necessarily with any reference to the main design, showing fine carved trailing floral patterns, often in definite sections and with a tiny border surrounding the designs. After c 1800 the guards changed from a floral design to depicting scenes from Chinese life or scenes with animals (often of dragons) in heavy raised carving and with no outlining border . . . however, a few floral designs carried on into the century.

By c 1800 Chinese ivory brisé fans suddenly changed to being carved on both sides of the ivory sticks—which meant that the ivory had to become rather thicker and therefore rather heavier. From c 1800 to c 1835 they became somewhat standardised: many were between 7 to 8 inches in length (16–19 cm); the finials of the sticks remained rounded, but bordering and fine inserts disappeared and the area above the ribbon became a sweeping continuation of the design below the ribbon; the gorge area became smaller and more stylised; the main body continued to be ribbed but had far more solid sections of ivory carved with designs showing scenes from Chinese life on both sides of the fan.

By c 1850 the Chinese ivory brisé fan suddenly declined in quality. The rounded finials flattened out, the carving on the sticks became coarse, crude and indistinguishable because it was so shallow: only the

guards were still worthwhile. Naturally these are generalisations on the evolution of the Chinese ivory brisé fan: there are of course exceptions, especially when a fan was made to order and not merely an impersonal export from Canton. For Japanese ivory brisé fans see ZŌGE OGI.
Illustration Nos. 6, 16, 17.

CHINESE LACQUER FANS

Lacquer fans were made in the East; fans made in the West which look as though they have been lacquered have actually only been varnished. The term 'lacquer fans' refers strictly to a short series of fine brisé fans from China which date from approximately 1790 to 1850. They are small, light, mainly coloured black and gold. Their decoration is almost always in three distinct sections: that above the ribbon (or, in rare cases, strong thread), that of the main 'leaf' and that of the gorge area. Usually each stick is straight except for a small curvature by the simulated gorge and usually each stick finial is curved like a fingertip. They rarely have loops added and the final throat of the guard near the rivet can be unbelievably slender. They are lacquered on to wood. In the main, in the earlier examples, the gold patterning on the black lacquer is of a delicate vine leaf while, towards the end of their popularity, figure and architectural subjects were introduced, some in lavish vignettes. They were generally both made in and exported from Canton.
Illustration Nos. XIII, 17.

17 a, b Chinese ivory brisé fan, finely pierced, lacquered with a scene of a bowl of flowers and two birds in the reserves (the design is identical on the reverse). It has it's original fine cording to hold it together at the top. Made for the European market. Probably late 17th century. Private Collection.

CHINOISERIE

This is a Western fashion of the seventeenth and eighteenth centuries, seen primarily in interior design, furniture, pottery, textiles and garden design, that represents a fanciful European interpretation of Chinese styles. In the first decades of the seventeenth century, English, Italian and, later, other craftsmen began to draw freely on decorative forms found on cabinets, porcelain vessels and embroideries imported from China. The earliest appearance of a major chinoiserie interior scheme was in Louis Le Vau's *Trianon de porcelaine* of 1670–71 (subsequently destroyed), built for Louis XIV at Versailles. The fad spread rapidly: indeed, no court residence, especially in Germany, was complete without its Chinese room, which was often, as it had been for Louis, the room for the Prince's mistress (e.g. Lackkabinett, Schloss Ludwigsburg, Württemberg, 1714–22). Chinoiserie, used mainly in conjunction with Baroque and Rococo styles, featured extensive gilding and lacquering; much use of blue-and-white (e.g. in Delftware); asymmetrical forms; disruptions of orthodox perspective; and Oriental figures and motifs. An entire chapter is devoted to chinoiserie in *Fans from the East*, detailing sources of design (Bérain, Pillement, etc.), difficulties for the fan makers and so on. Another invaluable source is the book on *Chinoiserie* by Hugh Honour. See also my own article on 'Chinoiserie and Japanning' in the *FCI Bulletin* No. 12 (Summer 1979).

Fans made in the chinoiserie style still continue to tease collectors, and many are incorrectly attributed, for the Chinese fan painters who exported fans to the West were very able indeed in interpreting the prevailing tastes. Some fan leaves were separately painted and sent to be mounted on Western sticks; some sticks were made in China from patterns sent out from the West (as they sent out designs for porcelain) and then mounted with Western leaves at a later date. On the other hand there were many equally clever Western decorators who copied Chinese fans or styles and sold them as Oriental in order to receive a better price.

For those who had never been to China (and very few had) the reports which filtered back described an idyllic civilisation. The 'vision of Cathay' evoked a mysterious, charming country, chronicled only by poets and painters; their subjects, apparently, were beautiful landscapes with craggy, snow-capped mountain ranges; grassy plains with cities of dreaming pagodas, intersected by meandering rivers; with

18. Chinoiserie fan in a glazed fan case. The chicken-skin leaf painted with eight shaped vignettes of Chinese figures, the reserves painted with golden trellis against a brown ground; the ivory sticks carved, pierced, silvered and gilt and backed with mother-of-pearl. French. $10\frac{1}{2}''$:26.5 cms. c 1780. (Fetched £260 in July 1982.) By courtesy of Christies, South Kensington.

whole fleets of delicate junks carrying fluttering pennants and precious cargoes which we can be sure contained jades, porcelain, silks, green ginger and delicately scented tea. The people of this land, according to their artists, seemed to be small and neat and all exactly alike, identifiable only by their rich, brocaded clothes. Work seemed forever at a standstill, apart from a few rustics who drowsed on the backs of water-buffaloes; life seemed eternally a warm afternoon, the employment of leisure apparently regarded as the serious business of life. They appeared to paint or write about a country of perpetual Spring, where the prunus was always in blossom and architects had created brightly painted latticed garden–houses to live in, jade pavilions, pleasure domes open to the sky, tall pagoda towers of porcelain and spindly little bridges over good-mannered streams. On the eaves, which were absurdly wide and turned up at the corners, hung tiny bells, set a–jingling by the reverberations of great gongs booming from nearby temples.

That is what was expected from 'Cathay' in the seventeenth and eighteenth centuries by the people of the West, and that is what the decorators supplied on goods (labelled 'chinoiserie' today—it is a nineteenth century term). So, to a certain extent, those scenes are more than slightly suspect when seen on a fan, especially if painted in tones of blue and white. Equally suspect is a scene where the figures all look one way, for while the Chinese enjoy painting a group of people, for instance, walking from the right to the left, they always have a final person on the left walking to the right in order to 'turn' the scene into a harmonious whole. Another clue to what is genuine Chinese (never Japanese), as against what came from the West, is that the Chinese did not paint upon skins but always upon paper or silk.

The whole subject is most tantalising and, without signatures or seal-marks, the best method of identification is to consult academics in the Chinese field and, even then, leave a small corner of your mind open. Illustration Nos. XVII, 18, 23.

CHOWRIES

The word means a 'whisk or fly-flapper', and can be spelled 'chowry' (this word first came into general usage in 1777) or the Hindi spelling of 'chaunri'—the proper name for the bushy tail of the Tibetan yak. Chowries were used in the Indian sub-continent from the beginning of time. In the Exhibition *Fans from the East* (and illustrated in the book of the same title) there was a very fine chowry made of ivory. As it was to be held in the hand it looked like a thin baton of solid ivory, carved with iris and poppy motifs from traditional Mughal miniatures, with a carved pineapple finial at the base, and at the other end it opened up like a vase. Into this vase were fixed hundreds of long, thin slivers of ivory—just as if a potato peeler had stripped off paper-thin lengths of the ivory straight from the tusk. These lengths were very tough and flexible, acting as small whips to any flies which settled. It was probably made for the Ruler of Patiala State in the eighteenth century, and is now in the Victoria and Albert Museum.

CHUKEI OGI

This fan is one of the commonest seen in the West and the type we most associate with the fan makers of Japan. It has simple bamboo sticks and a paper leaf which has been painted to fit in with one of the *No* dramas, and it is carried by an actor in the play. According to Neville Iröns, this type was first introduced in the seventeenth century. If you are able to read Japanese there is a very interesting section in Mr Nakamura Kiyoe's book on Japanese Fans, *Ogi to Ogie* (*Fans and Fan Painting*) in Chapter II, Part Two, where the author deals with (a) The unifying of the four companies and one style, (b) Fans of the *Shité*, (c) Fans of the *Waki*, (d) Resting of the Fan, and (e) Fans of the *Kyōgen*.
Illustration No. XXXIII.

CHURCH FANS

The first of the church fans appeared in England during the 1720s. They gave prayers, the Ten Commandments, the Creed, and special prayers for the Royal Family (unlike chapel fans). In the United States church fans, made from turkey feathers or palmetto leaves, were made available as you went in through the front door (and, in some places, still are). English church fans, printed mostly on paper, but occasionally on vellum or silk, had to have the sanction of the Bishop of London.

CLOUTÉ

This is a term which some auction houses use and tend to confuse the collectors in so doing. It comes from the French word *clou*, meaning a nail (hardware, not on the fingertip) and should mean, when used as a description, a form of 'nail-head' application, generally of metal.

One famous auction house uses the term 'clouté' as 'the application of a solid onto a solid, or encrustation'; i.e., carved ivory sticks may have a further decoration of carved mother-of-pearl set onto the top of the ivory, or even inlaid into a section of it but so that it is raised above the original background rather than being left flush with it.

Clouté always implies an extra ornamentation on top of something which was precious enough in the beginning. One famous collector considers clouté to mean the setting of a tiny solid silver figure onto the mother-of-pearl of a guard, or carved tortoiseshell motifs set onto ivory and so on. However, the simplest use of the term is the basic 'nail-head'. It is usually referred to as a European technique rather than the easily recognisable Oriental styles.

COCKADE FANS

This category encompasses fans of a particular shape rather than of a period or country. Basically the fan opens out into a complete circle, the end-sticks forming a long double handle. Some are made from textiles, paper or parchment, with a great many fine pleats, and others are brisé. The earliest known extant cockade fan (other than small terracotta models of ladies with cockade fans) is that said to have been owned by Queen Theodolinda (sixth century), now at Monza. Some very fine brisé cockade fans were popular from 1785, made from ivory, tortoiseshell, mother-of-pearl and aromatic woods.
Illustration Nos. 19, 20.

54

19. *Parasol cockade fan, made in Canton, of pierced ivory and with its original carved ivory hanging box. 15″ : 38 cms. c 1820. (Fetched £1100 in August 1981.) By courtesy of Christies, South Kensington.*

20 Souvenir fan, made
of olivewood, the
waxed cotton leaf
stencilled with
vignettes of floral
sprays, the leaf is
edged with a cotton
bobbin-lace border and
has a red cotton pull
tassel. The guard is
incised and decorated
with a marquetry inlay
of an Italian boy. An
oval mirror is set into
the reverse. Probably
made in Sorrento.
10″ : 25.5 cms. c 1870–
1900. Owned by Mrs
Georgette Tilley.

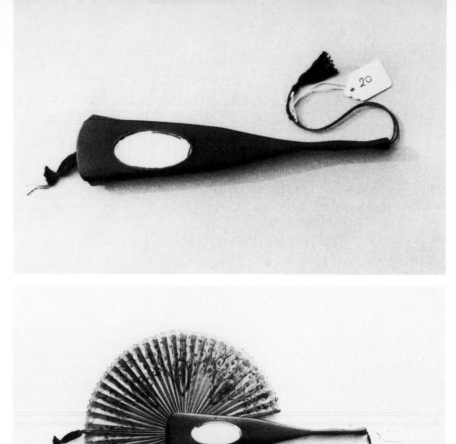

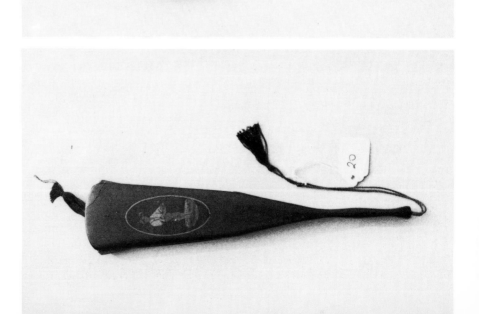

COMMEMORATIVE FANS

In the past these fans have been lumped into the category Advertising Fans; in some cases they do a double duty but the purest form should be hived off into their own section. They are fans which commemorate some event which is worth recording, from a cricket match between Eton and Harrow (a splendid extant example combines thick and thin paper with silk sections, silk tassels and sequins, and has a pencil attached) to a visit by a royal personage or even, as recently seen, 'General Booth's Welcome Home from Triumphal Campaign in the Far East, December 28th, 1926.' (Miller Collection). They have been known since printed fans began, yet most were made in the nineteenth century; earlier ones were more visual, with paintings of the event, while later ones were heavily over-printed with the facts worth recording. Materials ranged from paper and cardboard to silk and satin. They are not to be confused with advertising fans, although sometimes commercial companies did overprint them, possibly as a form of sponsorship. See AUTOGRAPH FANS, BALLOONING FANS, MARRIAGE FANS.
Illustration Nos. 21, 46.

21. The parchment leaf of this fan is printed with portraits of Queen Victoria at various ages and issued to commemorate her Diamond Jubilee; mounted on carved and painted wooden sticks. c 1897. English 10" : 25.5 cms. By courtesy of Bonhams, Knightsbridge.

CONVERSATION FANS

The 'language of the fan' is discussed elsewhere and, in most cases, could be expressed by means of any fan at all. However, there were some fans made in the eighteenth century with which a complete conversation could be carried on, by holding up the fan and then pulling back a tiny section, revealing a letter of the alphabet behind it. In this way it was possible to spell out each word without difficulty (so long as the viewer had excellent eyesight) rather than having to remember each fan 'signal'. It was a very leisurely way of flirting whilst a duenna was in tow and smacks of a much more pressure-free way of life. There is one in the Messel Collection.

DAGGER FANS

Dagger fans were used in the Orient, in both China and Japan, made by sword-makers as lethal weapons and eventually banned by law. They looked exactly like ordinary closed fans and could be thrust through an 'obi' or tucked into a boot. They were made from wood and came apart into two sections—pull the 'sticks' away and a sharp knife lay inside. Some people in Europe thought that they were made as paper-knives but this is incorrect, they were always made for murder. In Europe, especially in Germany and Austria, small 'daggers' were made of metal, with a velvet-covered sheath, which, when pulled apart, turned into fans acting on a 'half-cockade' principle. Both were novelties and the latter seemed to tie up with the Aesthetic movement. See an illustration of the latter on page 113 of *The Book of Fans*.

DANCE FANS

When, at last, ladies and gentlement danced together rather than as part of a set (contemporary with 'promiscuous seating' where ladies no longer sat at one side of a table facing the men but side by side with them) the gentleman invited the lady for a specific dance within a published programme of dances for the evening. Both sexes wrote down the name or number of the dance, and of the arranged partner— to avoid embarrassing discourtesies. Several types of fan were made to cater for this custom: firstly there were fans with numbered sticks on which the name could be written; then there were small brisé fans, complete with pencil, which would hang from the main fan, on which the names could be recorded; then there were tiny 'aide-memoire' fans

*22. Dance fan, the leaf of gauze embroidered with sequins and spangles to look like a
butterfly. French or English. Edwardian. With bone sticks set piqué point with cut steels.
The loop has an extra attachment from which a tiny dance programme would be hung.
8½" : 21.5 cms. Owned by Mrs Margaret Little.*

which were pulled out from the top of the guard; and lastly there
were ordinary paper booklets, complete with a tiny pencil, which
would be sold with the fan 'of a lady's choice' and which would hang
from the loop, nestling in the accompanying ribbons. In the main,
collectors like to have fans where the small pencil is still attached to
the fan. These were all made in Europe or the United States.
Illustration No. 22.

DECOUPÉ FANS
This is virtually the art of decorative paper or skin cutting and the
technique originated in China in the fourteenth century. The earliest

known illustrated European examples extant are the sixteenth century Cluny fan (now apparently lost) or the Oldham fan in the Museum of Fine Arts in Boston (others, not previously illustrated, are known to exist). They are made from fine vellum, cut out with tiny sharp scissors or with surgical knives (the latter type has the addition of small mica inserts to add to the effect of texturing). There were later copies of this technique in the seventeenth and eighteenth centuries. Another type of this work is a pricked design executed with pins or fine needles, giving a 'paper doyly' effect—in other words, the design looked like fine lace but the reverse was rough to the finger-tip. In a third type, the fan was mechanically punched out or stamped by paper-makers. I am grateful to Hélène Alexander for this information; Ref: Diderot: *Encyclopédie* section Découpeur et Gauffreur d'Etoffes en Planche lère; see Nos. 5 and 6—Fer à piquer autre fer à piquer on emporte, piece. In other words the paper makers had a mechanical punch which worked on alternate leaves and the work is recognisable as a technique.

23. Chinoiserie decoupé fan, the leaf finely painted with a Chinaman and fruit, the background decoupé with punched-work (possibly Chinese): mounted on carved mother-of-pearl sticks (the guards repaired). c 1760. 11″: 28 cms. By courtesy of Bonhams, Knightsbridge.

Another collector of note feels that this type of work was mostly carried out in China, using the 'fish-scale' motif (which is often seen in Chinese carving and piercing of ivory), probably also used with a small punch. In either category the paper decorator takes care not to interfere with any painted designs upon the leaf and works around it.

These fans were made in the various techniques mentioned above from the sixteenth to the nineteenth centuries.
Illustration Nos. XV, 3, 23.

DIRECTOIRE FANS

This type was made c 1789 to c 1805 and was the evolutionary link between the great, grand fans of the eighteenth century and the tiny Empire fans. They remain fairly large, are often made of ivory (brisé) or of embroidered textiles, and carry Neoclassical decorations. None of them have jewels but rely on slenderising lines and often reflect a post-Revolution 'serious' approach to life. See also NEOCLASSICISM, although not all Directoire fans carried Neoclassical motifs.
Illustration No. XXIII.

DOLLS' FANS

Small fans, exact replicas of fans for ladies, were provided for the exquisite dolls sold for children from c 1785 to the end of the Edwardian period. Nothing distinguishes them from adult fans other than their size.

DOMINO FANS

To attend a risqué play during the late seventeenth century and into the eighteenth, ladies were expected 'not to be there', in the same manner as Orientals in some high position who, on meeting a colleague, and with no time to spare for all the normal courtesies, would raise a fan across their face to say 'I am not here' . . . and no one would expect to be offended. Ladies would therefore go to the play with a mask, or domino, across their eyes. Later they carried fans with slits cut across for their eyes to watch the play, or which had small inserts of mica which acted as 'windows' for the lady to look through. During the nineteenth century some fans of this type were made, often of white silk or satin, with a black domino, edged with lace, set on a slant on the fan. See also MASK FANS, MICA FANS, GUT FANS.

EMBROIDERED FANS

The Chinese have always been famed for their superb embroidery techniques, sometimes so fine it was known as 'needle painting'. They made many embroidered fans on silk or satin, some of double but mostly single leaves, with the design so perfect that it is difficult to tell which is the obverse and which the reverse. They used, in the main, satin stitches (and Pekin knot on the many fan bags) and at least one fan is extant where there is fine embroidery on one side and the fan is painted on the other. In the East the embroiderers imitated contemporary paintings; in Europe the whole approach was that of exhibiting a craft, so that they used a great many types of stitches, i.e. gold thread tambour stitch on silk leaves, gold 'bearding' embroidery on Empire fans, etc. European embroidered fans were mainly produced in the nineteenth century; embroidered fans of China have been extant for much longer.
Illustration No. 4.

EMPIRE FANS

This period (c 1804 to c 1814) derives its name from the era during which Napoleon reigned as Emperor, starting in a simple enough manner and enriched as the years went by. Fashions for fans took a lesson from the Revolution and followed dress most carefully—they became, at last, a pure accessory—so where there were dresses of white muslin, batiste or embroidered cotton hugging the figure and slimming the silhouette, the fans followed suit. They were now small, even tiny, and were sometimes named 'imperceptibles' or 'minuets', but not 'Lilliputians' (q.v.). Fine paintings were 'out', sequins, spangles and gold net backing were 'in'—one is even known made from ass's hide. Sticks were made of less costly materials such as wood, horn and bone, some embellished with gold paint or cut steels. The leaves of nets (metallic or otherwise), silks or gauzes were decorated with sequins or spangles. The sequins are always circular (spangles are shaped), of gold, gold-colouring, silver or silver-colouring: they could become foxed in time and the real silver often turned black, leaving the cheapest type to remain bright today. Gold or metallic threads were used to embroider some Empire fans and there was the occasional use of paper-thin mother-of-pearl. The sticks were worked with care and guards occasionally had real gems randomly ornamenting them. Otherwise, in order

to break away and initiate something new (rather than imitating known decorations) marcasite was seen, as was jet, coloured glass, pastes, Wedgwood cameos or medallions and very colourful metallic backing foils. One special feature seen at this time was the 'barrel' rivet, and another was the fact that each fan appeared to have been made throughout by the same hand rather than piecemeal.
Illustration No. XXXV.

EUROPEAN IVORY BRISÉ FANS
Although a very great deal is known about ivory and the fact that it was carved in European countries, there still remains much controversy over whether ivory fans were carved in Dieppe, Paris, Holland or Switzerland. It is probable that they were carved in all these places and it is known that, early on, Chinese craftsmen were brought into Europe to carve ivory. During the nineteenth century some fine fans were made; those of the Empire period were often unbelievably fine (frequently with pastes or diamonds set at the rivet), and later there were many which were quite plain but had extremely heavy guards covered with carved flowers (possibly from Dieppe), or mountain goats in an Alpine scene (possibly from Switzerland), or with painted birds, insects and flowers along the edge, sometimes with straw or feathers applied (possibly from Holland). A vast field of research awaits exploration.

ÉVENTAIL
This is the French name for a fan. A fan maker is therefore an *éventailliste*.

FAN OF ONE THOUSAND FACES (See APPLIED FACES FANS)

FEATHER FANS
As explained in Chapter 1, these fans were probably the first type to be used and have continued to be popular ever since. Feathers can be used for brisé fans (especially during Edwardian times) with huge ostrich feathers (dyed or left plain) mounted on tortoiseshell sticks. Or feathers can be used to edge textiles, sandwiched between a double leaf. Or fans can be made from one huge wing of some bird—see page 52 of *The Book of Fans*, for an asymmetrical fan of eagles' feathers.

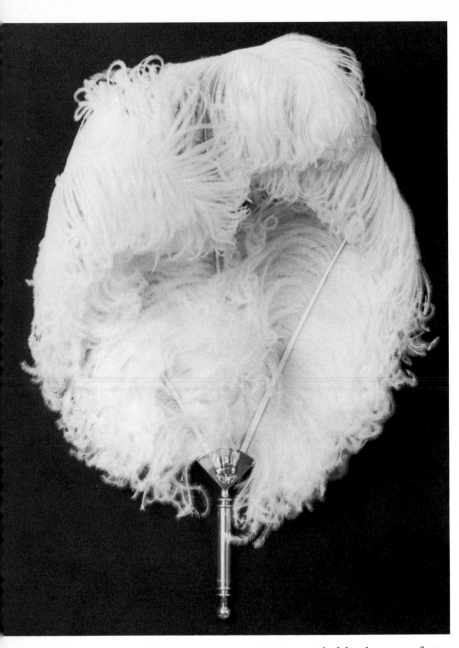

24. Commemorative fan, made by the Goldsmith and Jeweller, Tom Dobbie. Three pure white ostrich feathers, from the male bird, are held in a silver handle. This has an applied gold emblem showing the Prince of Wales' feathers set within a gold crown and the motto 'Ich Dien'. On the reverse is the logo of the Fan Circle International and the engraved words THE MARRIAGE OF THE PRINCE OF WALES AND LADY DIANA SPENCER 29 JULY 1981. At the base is the number within this Limited Edition of 25, plus the Hall marks. Overall height about 15″: 38 cms. Author's Collection.

There are many varieties, probably the most famous feather fans being those made to signify social position: those carried until recently on either side of the Pope; the sixteenth century fan made for Montezuma;

VI. Japanese ogi. A delicate painting in watercolours and inks of a landscape and three small figures. The sticks and guards are of ivory with takamaki-e incorporating shibayama inlay ; there is an engraved silver loop and twin silk tassels. This fan is very large and was extremely popular in both Europe and the USA c 1870. 13½" : 34.5 cms. From Fans of Imperial Japan *by Neville Irons, by courtesy of The House of Fans Limited.*

VII. Japanese ogi or folding fan. The leaf is of a silk and paper mixture and shows a scene of people in traditional costume against a harbour landscape. The sticks are of serrated bamboo, the ivory guards have a shibayama inlay. 10¾" : 27.5 cms. c 1875. From Fans of Imperial Japan *by Neville Irons, by courtesy of The House of Fans Limited.*

VIII and IX. *Gold filigree fan (18 carat), each stick having been hallmarked; it is also finely enamelled with white, yellow, blue and green. The mount is of Brussels Rosaline lace the silk tassel has a gold filigree cap. Possibly Spanish. 8″ : 20.5 cms. Owned by Mrs Georgette Tilley.*

X and XI. *Advertising fan, the paper leaf being hand-coloured and showing the Ironmongers Hall in Fenchurch Street (on the reverse their Arms). It would be interesting to know more about this fan as it was made by Duvelleroy, 167 Regent Street, W., and the writing is in French:* l'Hotel des Ferronniers dans la Rue de Fenchurch á Londres. *The sticks are of bone with a gilt decoration. Late 19th century. English. 10″ : 25.5 cms. Owned by Mrs Georgette Tilley.*

XII. Two fans from Java. Each is made from buffalo hide, held by carved buffalo horn. The brisé one on the left shows the normal Wayang shadow puppet designs carried out in gold and red (8″ : 20 cms): the fixed one on the right shows the Pertala Indera Maha Sakti, or stylised peacock (9¼″ : 23.5 cms). 19th century. Owned by Mrs Margaret Little.

XIII. Chinese lacquer brisé fan, made in Canton. 7¾″ : 19.75 cms. c 1840. Private Collection.

XIV. Varnished fan, European, possibly Dutch. This is a brisé fan, of ivory sticks, painted with a scene of 'Eliezer bearing gifts to Rebecca at the Well' and then varnished. This could also be called a 'Lilliputian' fan. 8" 20.5 cms. c 1740. Private Collection.

XV. Decoupé or Punched-work fan, the leaf showing a painted scene on paper with an elaborate background of punched-work (either French or Chinese). The ivory sticks are finely crafted and colourfully painted and varnished. 14½" : 37 cms. c 1760. Private Collection.

the fans made for Tutankhamun and those made for tribal chiefs in Borneo, parts of Africa and for the Indians in North America. Quite one of the most delightful is the fan made to commemorate the wedding of the Prince of Wales to Lady Diana Spencer in 1981. The celebrated goldsmith and jeweller, Tom Dobbie, made 25 of these, with silver handles, into which dropped three white ostrich feathers, similar to the insignia of the Prince. Permission had to be granted from the Royal couple that such a fan might be made, and it is known that the Princess was presented with one for herself. These fans will one day be great collectable items. They are numbered and dated, engraved with the commemoration details and have the logo of the Fan Circle International upon them, together with the hallmarks of the goldsmith, the London Assay Office and the year mark. It is a splendid link between the original material for fans (feathers) the ancient insignia of the Princes of Wales, the Fan Circle International and our future King and Queen. See COMMEMORATIVE FANS, OSTRICH FEATHER FANS. Illustration Nos. 24, 45.

FILIGREE FANS
There are several types of filigree fan. Basically the filigree is made of a soft (pure) silver or gold; the silver can also be gilt to prevent tarnishing and this metalwork is made by jewellers and sold by weight. They are delicate, valuable, impractical; many must have been melted down at times of financial stress and were probably made for presentation purposes.

The filigree was made in many countries: Norway, Malta, Italy, Spain and Portugal in the West, and China in the East. Some Chinese filigree fans also had enamels incorporated on them and 85% must have been exported from Canton.

Filigree was used in two distinct ways: for brisé fans, and as sticks for folding fans, occasionally interspersed by sticks made from other materials. The first fans of this category were made in China.
Illustration Nos. VIII, IX.

FLABELLUM
These fans are religious and can never be collected today. They have been written up at length in all the standard works on fans, but need hardly concern a collector in the 1980s.

FLAG FANS

In the Prado, in Madrid, there is a painting of Venus and Adonis by Paolo Veronese, where Venus is seen to be fanning Adonis as he sleeps, with a flag-shaped fan. (This painting is also to be seen on page 7 of that fine catalogue *Fans in Fashion*, an exhibition at the Fine Arts Museums of San Francisco in 1981.) Fans of this shape, as well as heart, spade and circular shaped, have also been made throughout the centuries in the Indian sub-continent. They are generally about 10 × 8 in (25 × 20 cm), with a stiff handle running down on one side. Some of them are single in construction, some double, with an inner lining. The handles can be simple polished wood or sumptuous solid silver or silver-gilt. The flag area may be made of a multitude of materials, from woven reeds or porcupine quills to peacock feathers or textiles . . . several known examples, made in the Indian sub-continent, are of cloth of gold.

In the main the flag-shaped fan would be hand-held. They have been seen in paintings from the thirteenth century and theories have been put forward that they may have been brought into Europe by returning Crusaders. They were very fashionable in Europe (especially in Venice) during the sixteenth and seventeenth centuries, but they occur far more frequently in Persian and Mughal miniatures and show what was in common use there over the centuries. Several fine examples were on show in the exhibition *Fans from the East*.

FLY-WHISK

Fly-whisks are as old as the fly. They are known worldwide throughout history: in the records of the Chapel of St Faith in the old St Paul's Cathedral in 1298 there is a mention of 'a muscatorium or fly-whip of peacock's feathers' and even in the 1980s various leaders of African countries carry one in the hand both for practical reasons and as a symbol of authority. See also CHOWRIES.
See illustration in *Fans from the East*, Plate 20.

FONTAGE FANS

This type of European folding fan was made *c* 1890 to 1935, the name delineating its shape. When open this fairly small fan appears to come to a point in the centre; when folded the fan leaf appears to zig-zag from the centre to the top of the guardstick. They were decorated

in the prevailing styles from Edwardian Rococo to Art Deco. See PAL-
METTO FANS, SHELL-SHAPED FANS.
Illustration No. XXI.

FOUR SCENES FANS

Normally a fan will open from left to right exhibiting a decoration
upon the obverse (front) which is finer (and shown outwards when
held), and another on the reverse which is seen by the holder. That
gives the owner, at most, two decorations (which are most often a
painted scene) upon a folding fan.

A 'four scenes fan' is generally a brisé fan, most popular *c* 1815, made
in Europe and the Far East from ivory, bone or horn. This small brisé
fan has a central section where there appears to be a crowding of sticks
behind the decoration in the centre. You can open it normally from
left to right and it shows two scenes. Then you can open it from right
to left and a third and even fourth scene appears on both sides. It is
done by a most elaborate form of ribboning by the maker.

It is possible to have the fans made in this style with a textile leaf
and, occasionally, the 'extra' scene turns out to be vaguely pornographic: the Chinese specialised in this. In Europe the decoration was
often Neoclassical in style, or with small baskets of flowers or figure
paintings, and the technique of 'half-painting' each stick in order to
provide four (or three) scenes was most exacting work . . . taking one
apart reveals great discipline on the part of the painter.

GLUE (See ADHESIVES)

GUMPAI UCHIWA

According to Joe Earle of the Victoria and Albert Museum, this is a
rigid handscreen owing its origins to the late Muromachi period
(1392–1568) and still used by the umpires at Sumo wrestling matches.
They were generally made of metal and a sharp tap with one would
soon part these giants.

GUNSEN

This is a 'war fan' which was first introduced in the Muromachi period
(1392–1568), all examples being very tough and durable. (Another
author dates this type back to the twelfth century.) The purpose of

25. *Gunsen, the gold leaf painted on both sides with the rising sun: mounted on iron sticks with the guard decorated with a dragon. Late 18th century. Japanese. 15″ : 38 cms. On the right a Tanto, dagger, in the shape of a cased fan. c 1800–1820. Japanese. 13″ : 33 cms. By courtesy of Bonhams, Knightsbridge.*

the fan was to signal, so it was carried by battle commanders. Normally the fan would have sturdy wooden or bamboo sticks, iron or brass guards and very thick (double) leaves. Neville Iröns tells us that the only decorative devices were the moon on one side (with a black background) and the sun on the other side (with a deep gold background). Illustration No. 25.

GUT FANS
During the first half of the eighteenth century some fans were made which consisted of a leaf created of knotted gut or horsehair. Almost

colourless, the gut is knotted in simple geometric patterns and applied across the sticks. Applied to this curious background (one noted collector has suggested it might have been a poor person's attempt to own a real lace fan) is a pattern of coloured paper or silk making designs of figures or 'lace'. These fans are rare and deserve deeper study. It has often been suggested that the majority were made in Germany.

Gut inserts were used in other fans as well, mainly during the eighteenth century. They were used where it seemed necessary to have an open 'window' for people to look through; one case is known where this 'window' is disguised as a birdcage. These gut inserts were quite small and must have been not only practical but a great novelty.

HANDSCREENS
This is another word for a rigid fan with a handle. It acts as a normal fan, it screens you from other people's sight or from the heat of a fire,

26. A pair of 19th century handscreens, the central vignettes decorated with three-dimensional birds made with beading and ringing; mounted on turned gilt sticks. c 1860. English. By courtesy of Bonhams, Knightsbridge.

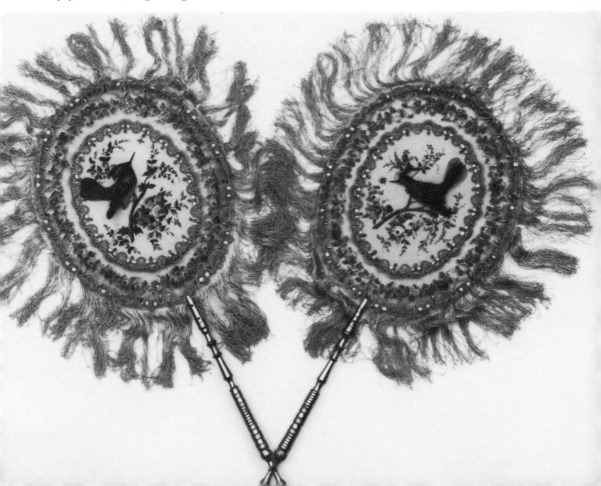

and it can be angled by some artificial means and used as an umbrella or sunshade. Handscreens have been used throughout history all over the world. See *Collecting Fans*, page 61.

European handscreens were heavier, more 'mechanical' than Eastern ones which were used personally as pure fans, whereas ladies in the West and the United States preferred a folding fan and used handscreens more to shield the face from a warm fire in an enclosed room. Illustration No. 26.

HI OGI

This is a very famous type of Japanese fan and is one of the earliest brisé types. Cypress wood is the normal material used, generally 38 sticks painted all over with gofun (powdered white lead) or gold and silver leaf and then decorated with painted patterns of flowers. The rivet is usually of metal, sometimes shaped like a bird, butterfly or bat, and the fan is held along the upper section by strong threads. On the guards, near the strong top, are suspended multicoloured cords plaited and twisted into various shapes. Mr Nakamura Kiyoe's book (see Bibliography) shows us, by means of a sketch, how this fan, when opened out by the Empress or one of her ladies, is wide enough for the cords hanging from the guards to fall just outside the width of the kimono and cascade to the ground unhampered.

HORN FANS

During the early nineteenth century (Empire period), horn fans became immensely popular. They pandered to the new taste for the simple, they were a spin-off from the prolific horn industry making gunpowder horns, and they were cheap.

During the Revolutionary period it was unfashionable to be seen wearing gold and silver brocades or diamonds, or carrying large painted and be-jewelled fans. Instead you carried a tiny horn fan, known as a 'minuscule' or 'imperceptible', decorated with non-controversial designs of painted flowers or cut-steels piqué—and the social classes could hardly be distinguished.

Horn has been used since the beginning of time. The historian, Theopompus, in the fourth century BC described the Kings of Paeonia (a territory in Northern Greece) drinking out of horns of great size, mounted with gold and silver rims. Since then, horn has been used for up to 180 useful articles such as spoons, beakers, the leaves for lanterns (light horns), shoe-horns, fans and so on. The almost continuous warfare of the Revolutionary period (c 1790–1815) encouraged the firearms industry and consequently there was a vast manufacture of containers for both gunpowder and priming instruments. They were made of horn, and the horn industry in Britain flourished.

Every part of a horn has been utilised, from the tips, curled over to make snuff-mulls, to the powder and shavings which are used as nitrogenous fertiliser. Horn is a natural plastic which can be worked in a multitude of ways and its shape altered through heating, carving and pressing. Man-made plastic was invented in 1862, (a form of cellulose nitrate called 'Parkesine' discovered by Alexander Parkes of Birmingham) as an attempt to copy horn more cheaply and using less labour.

There are, of course, many types of horn just as there are many types of synthetic plastic. Ox, buffalo, cow, sheep, goat and antelope horns are hollow and tough and can be split into flexible slices that can then be pressed into flat objects such as fan sticks. Rhinoceros horn is unique in that it is not hollow, has no grain and is very difficult to carve. These different qualities in the horns of various animals have led, to a certain extent, to special uses for each. Ox and goat horn were made into window panes and lantern plates before glass became generally available; deer horn was made into knife-handles, and beautiful ornamental work was usually created in buffalo horn.

Horn is non-absorbent, hygienic and has a wonderful tactile quality; it is unaffected by oils or mild acids and is not easily tarnished. Because of the presence of fibre in its structure, horn is truly a fibre-reinforced plastic. It is also biodegradable—when buried it eventually disintegrates, taking up to fourteen years to do so.

In Britain horn manufacturers was located at the termini of the cattle drives which ran the length and breadth of the country; the cattle were slaughtered and men were employed to de-horn the carcasses and clean the horns for the horn-traders, resulting in hornware craftsmen establishing their workshops conveniently near the slaughterhouses.

In the early 1700s a German named Humpersohn, inspired by the hornware made by the monks of Llanthony Abbey in Monmouthshire, set up the Abbey Horn Works close to a plentiful supply of the source of Herefordshire cattle in Gloucestershire. Humpersohn eventually sold the Abbey Horn Works to James Grove and Sons, horn button makers, and much later, in the 1920s, a new owner, Peter Leresche (of Huguenot descent) moved the business to Kendal, merging it with comb-makers—James Troughton and Sons. In 1955 John Barnes became its proprietor and Abbey Horn of Kendal, Cumbria, is a flourishing business today.

It seems certain that early nineteenth century horn fans were a by-product of the tremendous output of the comb industry. Most ladies then wore a minimum of three combs, one at each side of the head and one at the back; in 1851 the Aberdeen Combworks, to mention one place out of many, were employing more than 600 workers producing nine million combs a year in 1,928 different varieties.

Early in the seventeenth century the art of moulding and pressing horn was devised. One method was to place a piece of horn in a press, submerge it in boiling water (which softened it) and then to screw the press home to give a sharp impression of the dies. Later on horn was worked with gas, heating it in a soft gas flame to render it malleable, and meanwhile bending or twisting it to the required shape. The process is more critical than it appears, for horn has a 'molecular memory': if it is underheated it will slowly revert to its original shape; if it is overheated it will lose its strength and become brittle. Every horn has a different thickness and water content and has to be treated accordingly.

Once correctly shaped under heat the workpiece, such as a fan stick, is placed in a cool press in which it sets permanently into a required shape; on examination it appears that almost all early nineteenth-century horn fans were moulded in presses and not carved by hand; this includes any perforations. These horn fans of British manufacture embody the national preference for peaceful production rather than warlike attributes.

Early nineteenth-century horn fans were generally made from greenhorn, the word 'green' meaning that the horn was heated and plunged into boiling water (where it lost almost all its colour) until it was very soft and malleable, leaving the horn yellow-green in colour and translucent.

Finally there was a painstaking ritual of sanding and polishing to give the end-product the deep and lasting gloss that distinguishes high-quality hornware. One has to be careful not to confuse some forms of 'tortoiseshell' with horn because horn could quite easily be stained to emulate tortoiseshell. Tortoiseshell fans were far more expensive, but fakes can be recognised by the obviously even colouring on the sticks. The method used in the Victorian age was as follows:

Once the hornwork (such as the shaped and perforated fan sticks for a brisé fan) was ready it was softened by leaving it in a solution of one part nitric acid, two parts tannin, three parts wood vinegar and five parts tartar—or two parts wood vinegar, two parts tartar, two and a half parts zinc vitriol, three parts nitric acid and five parts tannin.

Then, to achieve a brown stain, you first painted on an aqueous solution of potassium ferrocyanide, allowing it to dry and then treating it with a hot dilute solution of copper sulphate.

A black stain was achieved by dissolving 50–60 grains of nitrate of silver in one ounce of distilled water—which looked colourless. A small brush was then dipped into the mixture and where a black stain was required (shading the brown into black) the mixture was painted on. When dry the horn was put into the sunshine, upon which the solution turned jet black.

One clue as to whether a fan is genuine tortoiseshell or fake dyed horn is that if the worker went to the expense of buying real tortoiseshell he would almost certainly use either silver or gold piqué on it; on fakes he would use cut steels. This was partly because cut steels were cheaper and partly because piqué work in shell is held by contraction when the shell cools, using no adhesives; horn does not react in the same way as tortoiseshell and therefore an adhesive *is* needed.

Horn fans were made all over the country and sold in local shops; there are records available from various shops (such as Alston and Greyhurst 'At the Blue Boar within Aldgate 1723'—now called Harvey and Gore in Burlington Gardens, London) where horn fans were sold in the early nineteenth century for a few shillings. The same fans sell today from £10 to £150 all over the land. Illustration No. XX.

IMPERCEPTIBLE FANS (See EMPIRE FANS)

ITA OGI
This is a Japanese type of fan, brisé, made from a great many sticks composed of either a fine wood or a bamboo, and then having a light design painted on them. The fan is generally held by a strong thread near the top of the sticks, sometimes in a decorative pattern, and gener-

ally has a metallic rivet. The sticks (which can be up to 48 in number) occasionally have gentle curves at the edges in the simulated gorge area. These fans can be very large indeed.

IVORY FOR FANS
Most people must be aware that the ivory used for fans is taken from the elephant. Although the teeth of the hippopotamus, walrus, narwhal, sperm whale and some types of wild boar and warthog are recognised as ivory they have little commercial value because of their size and (in some cases) lack of whiteness.

An elephant's tusk is the upper incisor and continues to grow throughout the lifetime of the male and female African elephant and of the male Indian elephant; the female Indian elephant has no tusks or only tiny ones. Elephant tusks from Africa weigh about 100 lb (45 kg) per pair; Asian tusks are somewhat smaller. There are two main types of elephant ivory: hard, usually from the Western part of Africa (and darker in colour), and soft.

All over the world ivory has a tremendous history of being carved and shaped, and fans made from ivory can be extremely fine and delicate. Techniques differ in various countries. Synthetic ivory is generally the use of bone (often the shin bones of horses) or, in the nineteenth and twentieth centuries, of plastics.

JAPANESE IVORY BRISÉ FANS (See ZŌGE OGI)

JENNY LIND FANS (See SHAPED-FABRIC FANS)

KOKOKU
These are Japanese advertising fans of the mid-nineteenth century onwards intended for home consumption. As with all advertising fans, very little attention is paid to the simple bamboo or wooden sticks; their purpose is to get across the advertised message and so the design on the leaf is extremely bold and colourful.

LACE
Lace has been used on fans since the eighteenth century; previous to that, there are sixteenth-century fans extant with decoupé work which imitated 'reticella' lace. Painted laces (on skin or paper) are also known,

27. A fan made in the Fabergé workshops of lace with tortoiseshell sticks and guards decorated with rose diamonds. By courtesy of Bonhams, Knightsbridge.

mainly because real lace was extremely expensive and, for a fan, it must also be shaped rather than made in a strip, cut to shape and turned in. Both needlepoint lace and bobbin lace were used for fans—the former always made by the professional—and finally machine-made lace was used. The year 1800 was quite a turning point because before that time the threads of lace were usually linen; after that time cotton was commoner. Also, laces were now made from silk and metal threads, and occasionally materials such as wool, aloe fibre and hair. Lace was made all over Europe, Russia and South America; it was not introduced into China until the nineteenth century and was not made there.

Only the finest laces are successful on fans, otherwise they appear too thick when folded . . . Chantilly looks delightful. During the eighteenth century lace fans had a leaf entirely made from the lace, often with a coat of arms worked into the design, while in the nineteenth century many fans were made as an amalgam of lace with gauze inserts, painted in pastel shades (or white upon black).

Because of the great expense of lace, the sticks and guards were made to set it off: fine lace is never mounted on cheap sticks. The best lace fans are made as a single mount; during the nineteenth century some lace fans were backed with silk or satin, sometimes as a contrast in colour and sometimes to act as a support. Nothing can look more feminine than a really fine lace fan of the eighteenth century, suitably mounted.

Illustration Nos. IV, VIII, XXX, 27.

LACE-BARK FANS FROM JAVA

The 'lace-bark' tree (*Lagetta lintearia*) originated in the West Indies but was introduced (by the Dutch) to Java during the nineteenth century. It produces a netting-like substance, almost like a net curtain, which has on occasion actually been used for clothing—there are two child's bonnets made from this in the Museum at Kew Botanical Gardens in London. In the *Fans from the East* exhibition, a brisé fan was shown using the 'lace' as long ovals on each ivory stick, strengthened all along the edges by what looked like a border of brown paper. In fact this was flat sections of 'Spatha', the sheath of the fruit of the Mountain Cabbage Palm.

Another strange material formed the tassel, made from the fibre of the pineapple plant, and this was brushed out, as well, to a floss-like texturing, to edge the tips of each brisé section. As an extra decoration delicate dried and pressed ferns were glued across the 'leaf' area.

Two more can be seen on pages 120/121 of *The Book of Fans*: the first in shades of cream, the second in shades of rich brown, with tortoiseshell sticks. Examples are known from both Jamaica and Indonesia, generally made in the nineteenth century.

LACQUER

This is a well-known term for coloured and frequently opaque varnishes applied to metal or wood, forming an important branch of decorative art, especially in Asia. Lac is the sticky resinous secretion of the tiny lac insect, *Laccifer lacca*, a species of scale insect: the word *lac* comes from the Persian word *Lak* and the Hindi word *Lakh*, both of which mean 'hundred thousand', indicating the vast number of the minute insects required to produce lac. In fact about 17,000 to 90,000 insects are needed to produce one pound of shellac. Lac is the basis of some but not all lacquers; in China and Japan it is the sap of the tree *Rhus vernicifera* which, cleaned of impurities, can be used in its natural state. The characteristic constituent of lacquer is called *urushiol*, from the Japanese *urushi*. The names of great lacquer artists are extremely well recorded in both China and Japan.

The base of Chinese and Japanese lacquer is nearly always wood, generally a pine having a soft and even grain; it is extremely thin and in artistic lacquer work is coated with a great many successive layers of lacquer, among which is a layer of hempen cloth or paper. Because each layer takes up to 24 hours to dry, the entire process of producing a surface suitable for an artist to decorate requires at least 18 days. The design may first be made on paper or drawn directly on the object with a thin paste of white lead or colour. Tiny bits of gold and silver may be applied with quill, bamboo tube or pointed tool. Long hardening periods are again necessary during this decorative stage.

In Europe the basic ingredient of varnished surfaces was shellac. Lacquer on fans produces some superb effects (black and gold, silver and gold, red and gold, etc.) and ensures that a fan remains extremely light. It is rarely cheap and often underrated

Many books have been written on both Chinese and Japanese techniques of lacquering and in the world of the fan the biggest accent is placed upon nineteenth-century Japanese fans with gold lacquerwork known as either *takamaki-e* or *hiramaki-e*. The addition of *shibayama* inlay brought Japanese fans to a decorative peak. *Shibayama* work is named after a Japanese family who worked with lacquer (especially on inro) during the eighteenth and early nineteenth centuries, adding tiny sections of carved semi-precious stones into the lacquer. They produced magnificent (thick) ivory guards brilliantly decorated with an elongated scene of a garden, perhaps, with cranes and bamboo leaves in gold lacquer and tiny flowers of carved mother-of-pearl, birds of carved agate and insects of carved jade. Some of these Japanese ivory fans were left quite plain, confining all the rich decoration to the guards: others showed superb gold lacquering (in various subtle colours) right across the brisé sticks. In each case the fan became so heavy it was almost impractical to use but was given as a most acceptable gift.

Illustration Nos. I, VI, 1.

LEATHER (See PARCHMENT)

LILLIPUTIAN FANS

There appears to be absolutely no reason to use the name 'Lilliputian' when describing 'Empire' fans, but to ascribe it to the very small fans of the early eighteenth century instead. It is known that fans were thus named, but the Victorian date is incorrect. *Gulliver's Travels into Several Remote Nations of the World* was written 1721–25 and published in 1726, the author being Jonathan Swift. At that same period there were two distinct forms to fans: that of large vellum or paper fans with an extravagant spread, and that of very small brisé fans; these brisé fans have never been successfully explained before except by being named (incorrectly) 'Vernis Martin' fans. In the past Victorian writers named Empire fans 'Lilliputian', but the title sits far more comfortably in the 1720s when *Gulliver's Travels* was actually written. Therefore, to my mind, early eighteenth-century varnished brisé fans should be named 'Lilliputians'. See also VARNISHED FANS.

Illustration Nos. VIII, XIV.

LOOFAH FANS

I have recently come across the same type of fan made in both Thailand and in remote villages up the Amazon River. They are the conventional brisé type, the upper half being decorated with white ducks' feathers edged with maribou, and with an over-decoration of small, brilliantly coloured parakeet feathers. The curiosity is in the stick area, for the very few, broad, light 'sticks' are made from dried loofahs: they were identified for me as 'Cucurbit', a member of the cucumber family, by the Museum at Kew Gardens in London. It is indeed strange to have sticks made from dried sponges, but they are light and strong and carry out their purpose perfectly adequately.

See an illustration in *Fans from the East*, Plate 24.

LOOPS

The use of a loop attached to the rivet of a fan came in, as a general rule, in the late 1830s. Some have actually been seen from the eighteenth century but are extremely rare and must have been a novelty.

Loops were brought in then because a lady had just too many things to carry and, especially when dancing in the new (modern) style, when both hands were occupied for the first time, she could suspend her fan temporarily over her wrist and immediately have it to hand at the end of each dance.

Loops have been made of many types of metals from gold to a base metal. In the East some magnificent ones are extant and in the West there are some made with real gemstones. They are purely for the ribbon to pass through and are not part of the construction of a fan. See also PARTS OF A FAN and RIVETS.

LORGNETTE FANS

In the past, people who had bad eyesight did not advertise the fact if they could possibly help it; instead they set a magnifying-glass in the most solid part of the guardstick of a fan, or within the rivet area. These fans were seen during the eighteenth century, but as spectacles were used more and more in the nineteenth century there was no more need for them. They are also called 'Quizzing fans'.

MACAO FANS (See APPLIED FACES FANS)

MAI OGI

These are fans used by the Japanese in the dance. When fans have to be in movement with the body (as opposed to being merely waved while the owner is seated) the consideration of balance is of great importance. Fans must be lighter than normal but extremely strong. Most dance fans therefore have only a few supple but strong bamboo sticks which support a single leaf of painted paper or textiles such as silk or satin. Their distinguishing feature is their guards: to keep that balance the guards are either divided into two segments, attached to the end pleat (all the pleats are wide) with matching silk cords, or there are two slender outer 'sticks' attached by cords. These fans appear to have first made themselves a special category from the seventeenth century but those which appear in sales are now almost always nineteenth century . . . an earlier purchase would be a great coup.

MANDARIN FANS

The term 'Mandarin Fan' came to be used, incorrectly, during the nineteenth century, to describe Applied Faces Fans. The Victorians did not realise that the latter were made for export only and assumed that, because a fan showed mandarins in its design (complete with tiny ivory faces), it had been made expressly for the use of a particular mandarin.

True mandarin fans were made to match the clothes of their owners, unless they were a special 'gift' fan, and had designs on them to indicate their status at court. They were specially made to order and were not for sale to the public. See also APPLIED FACES FANS.

MARRIAGE FANS

Another name is a 'Bridal' or 'Wedding' Fan, but 'Marriage' encompasses all the facets of this type. Brides in the past used to have a selection of fans to give out to their attendants or special friends as a commemorative gift. Husbands-to-be used also to commission fine fans for their brides: some were ivory brisé fans with a central cartouche with the bride's monogram carved upon it (or a double one, especially when a coronet of some type was incorporated); others were especially painted with some significant scene.

Another form of marriage fan was some fine fan which was commissioned for the bride and given as a wedding present. In many of these there are portraits of both bride and groom in the design. Various members of Royal families have gone to great expense with these fans and other noble families were never far behind. The decoration generally refers to 'the state of marriage': i.e., some reference to the god Hymen, 'true lover's knots', putti and cupids, hearts and flowers, and so on. None of them set out sternly to instruct, all of them were made to delight and to enhance the happy occasion. They are exclusive, personal and occasionally very rare, but they are only of real importance and interest if the entire provenance is attached and you are furnished with the names of the people and the date.

In the United States today there has again developed a very pretty notion of using marriage fans. Mrs Geraldine Pember in California organises marriages for certain families where the bride carries a white fan with white ribbons and flowers and her attendants all carry matching fans with contrasting ribbons and flowers suitable to their dresses. Illustration No. XXXVI.

MASK FANS

There is a certain very specialist group of fans known as the 'Mask fans' which all appear to have come from the same stable during the first half of the eighteenth century. Basically the fans have a very large mask printed or painted across the leaf with the eyes cut out, and it seems that they were made for ladies going to the theatre. Less than ten are known: four are on display (the Metropolitan Museum, New York; the Museum of Fine Arts, Boston; the Fine Arts Museums in San Francisco; the Kremlin in Moscow), and I know of three others in private collections. Miss Esther Oldham researched her extremely early one over a period of ten years (now in the Museum of Fine Arts in Boston) which has laid very valuable ground for all the others— details are on pages 119–127 in *The Book of Fans*. Some authors refer to this type as 'Peeping fans', especially as John Gay, in his poem 'The Fan', written in 1713, refers to them thus:

> The Peeping Fan in modern times shall rise,
> Through which unseen the female ogle flies.

It is extremely interesting to find that each fan in this specialist category is slightly different in some way: the painted Oldham version appearing to have the fullest collection of illustrations which were inspired by *The Beggar's Opera*, the others (later) in somewhat the same style and taking at least one of the vignettes, while adding other small scenes from contemporary life. It is indeed a teasing type of fan: as much research has been done on this fan as in any other category, yet this very fact has acted as a red rag to a bull and various 'authorities' have attempted to destroy its validity. Why? If any fact is disputed then surely it would be better openly discussed? The type is so very rare it would be a greater service to collectors to illustrate them all and encourage each owner to research his own and publish his findings. This will never happen, of course, but it would be the ideal solution.

MEDALLION (See CARTOUCHE)

MEN'S FANS
In the East various fans were made with a perfectly plain leaf (or brisé sticks) so that the male owner might have something available on which to write notes; fans for ladies always had some form of decoration as it was generally agreed that ladies would not be required to write anything.

In Europe it is known that men, especially in Court circles, carried fans in the eighteenth century. Some people believe that men carried brisé fans, others think they carried large, plain fans; still others assert that they carried fans with small insects painted upon them. All this is pure speculation and there is simply no evidence at present to prove whether there was a special category of fans for men or whether they carried any fashionable fan of the period. Provenance is needed before there is proof. It is, however, generally known that early in the eighteenth century it was said that there were three sexes, men, women and Herveys—referring to Lord Hervey, who appeared to be sexually ambidextrous. He always carried a fan and was laughingly known behind hands as 'Lord Fanny'.

MICA FANS

Mica is the name given to a group of minerals which include muscovite (potash mica) and phlogopite (magnesia mica). It is found in igneous rocks and splits in one direction only. It can therefore be foliated into very thin sheets which are tough and elastic, do not break easily but can be marked with the fingernail. It is mined in large blocks and then split to the desired size with sharp knives.

Mica is an easy material to split into very fine sections and it is also possible to cut it with scissors into patterns. It has often been used as an added material for a fan and it is proof of its strength that some very fine late seventeenth century fans remain intact. It has been used in both the East and the West for four centuries.

There is one extremely interesting group of unique late seventeenth century fans (see page 170 of *A Collector's History of Fans*) of which only four are known, all apparently by the same hand. They are normal folding fans, set on ivory or tortoiseshell sticks with the decoration arranged in three tiers across the sticks to form the leaf. This decoration consists of tiny rectangular sections of paper-thin mica panels set into paper or braid frames and having detailed paintings of busts, flowers, birds or dogs on each. None of these fans is exactly the same (one has to search for the differences) but they are obviously from the same 'stable'. Here, the maker, who may have been Dutch, does not apparently use the mica for its transparent properties but as a smooth and unusual surface on which to paint.

Another very early and interesting fan, made in China for export to South America, c 1700, shows Phillip V of Spain. Then there are others where large masses of mica have been used, lightly painted (in some cases with animals of the Zodiac).

28. Mica fan, made in the Orient. There is a brightly painted paper leaf with mica inserts forming animal creatures from Chinese mythology; pierced ivory sticks, the guards painted in reds and greeny-greys, terminating in a reversed tulip-shaped finial and having a domed metal pivot. Late 17th century or very early 18th century. Private Collection.

During the eighteenth century mica was quite often used as inserts into a scene for a peeping or quizzing fan, or with chinoiserie designs such as the magnificent 'palace' scene in the Messel Collection where mica is set as 'windows' with courtesans looking out (see Plate 15 in *Fans from the East*). The special quality of mica for fans is the fact that the mica does not appear transparent from the front, it just seems a part of the overall design. Once held up to the face, however, the transparent sections all too obviously have their uses.

On the whole mica fans are very much sought after and extremely expensive; they do not often change hands, either.
Illustration Nos. 9, 28.

MINUET FANS (see EMPIRE FANS)

MITA OGI

These Japanese fans are for processions and are huge in size. (Some were also used on the stage.) The general effect is obtained by decorating the leaf with bright colours and leaving the wood or bamboo sticks quite plain. Quite often the leaf is of fine linen rather than paper. They were most used in the nineteenth century.

MONOGRAM FANS

During the nineteenth century it was very appealing to some people to apply monograms, arms, crests, etc., upon a fan in their own homes. The fans were made of sycamore wood, brisé, with wide sticks and, naturally, perfectly plain; some were made in Austria or Bavaria. It was then possible to buy sheets of tiny monograms, etc. from a dealer, e.g. J. H. Kent & Co., Dealers in Crests, Monograms & etc. of 3 Edward Terrace, Cardiff, and cut them out and apply them to your fan. It was more normal to buy especial albums for this purpose; for example, Marcus Ward & Co. Ltd. (Copyright Entered at Stationers Hall) produced small books entitled *Armorie—An Album for Arms, Crests and Monograms*. Upon each facing page would be some form of lightly printed design, such as an outline of a church window which had spaces to infill with the monograms of Bishops. There were pages for the Arms, Crests or Monograms of the Army Regiments, Mercantile Houses, Insurance Companies, Dukes, Towns, the Navy, Earls, Schools, Clubs, Colleges in Universities, Hotels and well-established Overseas Clubs. The entertainment provided was to collect sufficient of each type, cut them out and tastefully arrange them in patterns on the correct illustrated page.

During the nineteenth century people also decorated screens and scrap-books, and it was known that some applied scraps to china, wood or leather objects and to the glass balls which hung on Christmas Trees when they were first in vogue; the art was called 'Decalcomania', from 'decals', meaning 'transfers', and meant the decorating and labelling of any object that cannot be run through a press (see *The New Encyclopaedia Britannica*). One is tempted to call these fans 'Decalcomania Fans' but 'Monogram Fans' would be more readily understood. According to the 1864 *Englishwoman's Domestic Magazine*, another supplier of monograms was Barnard & Sons, 339 Oxford Street, London.

These fans were made from *c* 1850; the basic sycamore fan was also used to paint at home with your own pattern, and others are known from Vienna with white flowers painted upon a red or blue background. The practice of putting monograms, etc., into albums then spread to collecting stamps and putting *them* into albums. As the postal system was rapidly increasing worldwide, and monograms were becoming less interesting because they were already established, monogram fans gradually faded out. See illustration on page 83 of *The Book of Fans*.

MONTGOLFIER FANS (See BALLOONING FANS)

MOTHER-OF-PEARL
Technically this material should come under the heading 'Pearl' or 'Nacre' (from the Arabic *nakar*). It is a material often used in fine fans for sticks and guards and occasionally crushed and used as a mosaic on leaves as well. Early mother-of-pearl came in short pieces which can be seen to be spliced in several sections in order to lengthen them along a stick or guard: because the material is so expensive and difficult to work (it splits very easily), you rarely find an extension of a mother-of-pearl stick made of pearl but from bone or wood instead, secreted between two leaves. The white pearl came from Madagascar, the black pearl from various areas in the East and the 'burgauté' pearl, sometimes also known as 'goldfish', from Japan. This latter has been used in some of the finest fans as a fragile and extremely thin backing for further overlaid designs, sensuous as exotic shot-silk, or winking its rainbow lights from within carved guards. On occasions mother-of-pearl is discovered clouté on wooden or ivory sticks, showing delightful little figures from the Comedia dell'Arte, and attached to the backing material with tiny silver pins.

Mother-of-pearl brisé fans were made in the Orient, notably in China, mainly for export purposes from Canton. In the nineteenth century they came carved on both sides (etched might be a better word) and, according to Neville Iröns in *Fans from Imperial China*, 'from trade labels it appears that a number of specialists existed, foremost Hoaching, followed by others such as Shongshing.'

Mother-of-pearl carved work is never cheap; only when it was machine-made and dyed to pastel shades in the nineteenth and early twentieth centuries did the material become slightly debased and its character altered. A great deal of care must be taken over the material when repairing it.

Illustration Nos. IV, V, XXX, XXXVII, XL, 1, 15, 23, 39.

MOURNING FANS

There are two types of mourning fan: those where an 'ordinary' scene is painted in pale greys, black and white ('en grisaille'), and those where there is a definite 'mourning' scene (classical in essence) with weeping women, weeping willows, funerary urns, etc. The sticks for both are simple, uncoloured, sometimes lightened with silver. During Victorian times many fans were made from plain black satin with black painted sticks; some were for ladies in mourning, others were made because mature ladies never stirred from the use of black in their costume, especially in Spain and Italy.

However, in 1874, Mary Reed Bobbit wrote of the immense painted black satin fans: 'These big fans are all the fashion in London, nobody carries anything else.' So one must not always assume that black satin meant 'mourning', for this was the age of contrasts in dress.

All the same, when in mourning there were very strict rules: a widow wore full mourning for two years (and sometimes for longer); as a parent (or for a parent) for one year; for a brother or sister for six months and for all other relatives for three months.

NEAPOLITAN FANS

In the exhibition 'Fans and the Grand Tour' (Brighton Museum, 1982) a fine collection of Neapolitan fans was displayed with all the 'correct' background material of carved cameos, small bronzes, fine paintings, miniatures, mosaics and copies of books which would have accompanied a wealthy young man as he travelled the Continent.

During this intriguing tour of the Continent a great many souvenirs were bought and shipped back to England, partly as proof that the 'grand tour' had been undertaken at all and partly as presents to give away. Smaller articles such as fans were ideal as gifts, partly because they were 'the latest thing' in use in each country and partly because they were a pictorial commemoration of various places. The most interesting events were the series of eruptions of Vesuvius outside Naples, and many fans were painted to show these and/or the City and Bay.

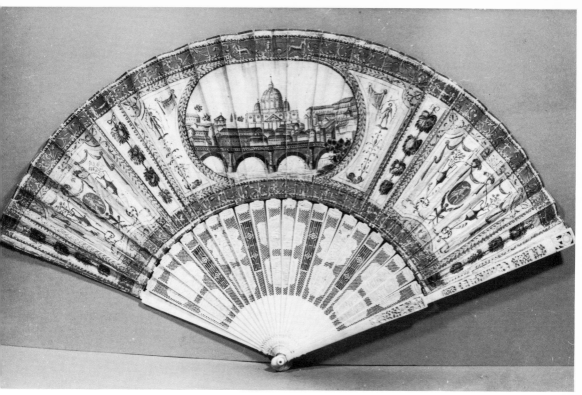

29. Grand Tour fan of high quality. The chicken-skin leaf is painted with a view of Rome and the Tiber, further decorations derived from Herculaneum and Pompeii; ivory sticks pressed and pierced, the guards carved and pierced. The colours of the leaf are of bands of turquoise at top and bottom, all the framing in pink and the ground a primrose yellow. Italian, $11\frac{1}{4}''$: 28.5 cms. c 1785. Owned by Mrs Pamela Hudson.

Neapolitan fans were made from c 1760 onwards. Some are printed, some painted, many with fine sticks crafted in separate ways and some with an application of coral on them (or simulated coral) to publicise a local craft. Illustration No. 29.

NEOCLASSICISM
This is a taste for classical serenity and archaeologically correct forms that began to be perceptible c 1750 and flourished in all branches of the visual arts from c 1780 until the mid–nineteenth century. In Europe it represented a reaction against the excesses of the last phase of the Baroque and was symptomatic of a new philosophical outlook. As the Baroque had been the style of Absolutism, so Neoclassicism corresponded loosely to Enlightenment and the Age of Reason, represent-

ing an attempt to recreate order and reason through the adoption of classical forms. Coincidental with the rise in Neoclassicism and exerting a formative and profound influence on the movement, was a new and more scientific interest in classical antiquity. The discovery, exploration, and archaeological investigation of classical sites in Italy, Greece and Asia Minor was crucial to the emergence of Neoclassicism.

Neoclassical fans mean those which have some reference in their decoration to the movement from c 1780 to c 1830. These fans are also often marked by having straight sticks (generally pierced to lighten the weight and design), as the excesses of the Rococo were also frowned upon at that time. Some extremely fine fans were made and enormous trouble seems to have been expended on getting every tiny detail correct. See also DIRECTOIRE FANS
Illustration No. XXXV.

OGI (SENSU)

This type of fan was made by the Japanese for the export market after 1860. It generally has a double leaf of paper, or a mixture of paper and silk, or a very fine linen which has been sized. On this leaf is a well-painted scene from a multitude of different subjects showing life in Japan both in and out of doors. The sticks are generally of wood, bamboo or ivory with absolutely no decoration at all, except for the fact that many have serrations along the edge. The guards can be of a contrasting material and can be lavishly decorated with shibayama or lacquer. It is of interest to discover how many of this type, with ivory guards, have an added ojime (bead) on the tassel. The making of these beads, associated with netsuke and inro, was an art in itself. Their purpose was to keep the cords of the tassel untangled.

OSTRICH FEATHER FANS

The use of ostrich feathers has been known since the beginning of time; many people were intrigued to hear of Tutankhamun's gold and ostrich feather fan found in his tomb, the ostrich feathers being perfect until exposed to the light and air when they disintegrated into dust. When they began to be used in the nineteenth century, female ostrich feathers were seen first as a full spread. There is a publicity photograph in an 1888 issue of *Woman's World*, showing Madame Patti in the newest fashions, using a female ostrich feather fan. Ladies took to wearing two or three ostrich plumes (normally white) in the hair from 1794–1797 and then, slightly modified, carried on as 'Court Dress' into the twentieth century. As a result of this and the use of ostrich feathers in hats and on fans, ostrich farms were established in South Africa, the Southern United States, Australia and elsewhere—but the trade collapsed after 1918. Brown, or brown and white feathers are from the female bird; black or pure white are from the male. The white feathers dyed very well to a multitude of pastel shades. In the twentieth century many fans were carried with either a single feather, or two, placed in a short fan-holder and dyed to match a special dress, often shading in tone.

PALMETTO FANS

This type was made as a European folding fan *c* 1890–1935. They appear in shape, when open, as a sweeping curve with a slightly flattened central section. When closed they have a zig-zag outline of the leaf to the guard, like the 'Fontage Fans'. See also FONTAGE FANS, SHELL-SHAPED FANS.

PANORAMA FANS

In the past, every attempt was made to amuse ladies of fashion, and this type of fan was the forerunner of the cinema. The idea was to watch changing pictures in the centre of a fan by looking through a central window of a handscreen. Behind this window were two rolls of ivory or wood which were turned round by a handle positioned at the side. Over these rolls was placed a continuous piece of paper on which was painted a variety of scenes which were wound on from one roll to another (like a film spool in a camera). They were made from the mid-eighteenth to the mid-nineteenth centuries. Sheila Smith of Sheila Smith Antiques, Bath, once showed me an extremely rare, matching pair of eighteenth century panoramic fans with turned ivory handles and scenes of Versailles Palace. See also TOPOGRAPHICAL FANS.

PARCHMENT

This material, upon which writing or painting is inscribed, consists of the processed skins of certain animals, chiefly sheep, goats and calves. The name apparently derives from Pergamum (modern Bergama, Turkey) where parchment is said to have been invented in the second

30. English Fan, the vellum leaf decorated with a central stipple engraved vignette, mounted on pierced and carved ivory sticks. c 1800–1810. 10½" : 26.5 cms. By courtesy of Bonhams, Knightsbridge.

century BC. Skins had been used even earlier as a writing material but a new, more thorough method of cleaning, stretching and scraping made possible the use of both sides of a manuscript leaf.

Parchment made from the more delicate skins of calf or kid, or from still-born or newly born calf or lamb, came to be called 'vellum', a term that was broadened in its usage to include any especially fine parchments.

Fan leaves have been made of various forms of parchment, especially vellum in Europe. Asses' hide has been known as a material, as has the leather from the chamois. In the Far East there are many fans made from buffalo hide but, as far as is known, the Chinese did not use any form of skin for their fans. See also SHADOW FANS FROM JAVA.
Ilustration Nos. 2, 12, 21, 30, 34, 40.

PARTS OF A FAN

All the parts of a fan are made to relate to another part and to become a balanced whole. A folding fan is created from two main sections: the leaf and the sticks. This leaf can be made from any material which will fold, and it is set upon the sticks, usually upon the upper half, leaving the lower parts to be decorated in some way; the uncovered part of the sticks is also known as the 'blade'. The uncovered part of the stick is then divided into sections: the shoulder at the leaf end,

90

the gorge or shoulder in the centre and the head at the end. This head area of the fan is of great importance, because in the centre you find a rivet, pierced right through, around which the pivot revolves. This rivet is very often made from metal, sometimes having a form of button to protect each end. The entire fan is then protected by the guards or guardsticks, which are generally much the same as the sticks themselves, only wider.

In France the entire stick area is *la monture*, the sticks are known as *brins*, the leaf or mount is called *le feuille*, the head area is termed *rivure* and the guardsticks are called *panaches*.

In this book I use the simplest terms of 'leaf', 'sticks', 'guards' and 'rivet'. See also LOOPS and RIVETS.

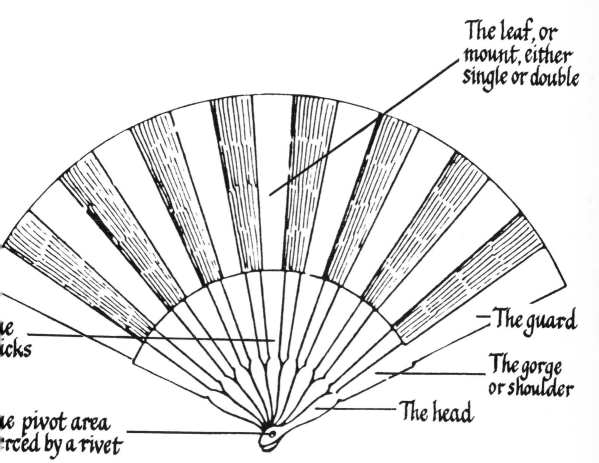

The leaf, or mount, either single or double

The guard

The gorge or shoulder

The head

...e ...icks

...e pivot area ...rced by a rivet

31. a&b Victorian fan, the leaf of black satin, painted with a flower design. The sticks and guards are of a black wood, the guards containing two sliding compartments; one having sewing implements and, below, a vinaigrette (inscribed PATENT in gold lettering): the other guard containing a comb and nail-file and, below, a small oval mirror. The tassel opens and probably housed a thimble. See Bertha de Vere Green's book, page 287. English. Private Collection.

PIEN-MIEN

The word *ogi* in Japanese means a 'folding fan'; the word *uchiwa*, a fixed fan. In Chinese the word *pien-mien* means a fixed fan which could be conveniently held in the hand 'to agitate the air'. Therefore

32 Three Chinese pien-mien of the late 18th century. Top: very finely painted with two Chinese ladies in a garden; Chinese calligraphy on the reverse: mounted on a lacquered handle. 15″: 38 cms. Bottom: a matching pair with Chinese figures in a landscape on a gold ground; the reverse (as seen on the left) decorated with birds and flowers made from kingfisher feathers; mounted on carved and pierced ivory handles. 15″: 38 cms. By courtesy of Bonhams, Knightsbridge.

it is a very overall term. There are some superb pien-mien to be seen in the Messel Collection, from betel palm stretched over finely split bamboo to K'o-ssu, i.e. shadow embroidery on silk (see an illustration of the former in *Fans from the East*, number 3, page 31; for the latter, see page 125 of *The Collector's Book of Fans*).
Illustration No. 32.

PIQUÉ-WORK
This is a decorative technique, usually employed on tortoiseshell or ivory, in which inlaid designs are created by means of small gold or silver 'pins'. The art reached its highest point in seventeenth and eighteenth century France, particularly for the decoration of small articles such as fans, combs, patchboxes and snuffboxes.

Both tortoiseshell and ivory are animal products of great versatility and both slightly expand when hot and contract when cold. In order to decorate tortoiseshell with piqué-work a fan guard, for instance, is completely finished off and then a pattern is very lightly inscribed on the surface and tiny holes are drilled. The shell is then carefully heated over fine quality smokeless charcoal and either pure gold or pure silver rods are inserted into the tiny holes. When the shell cools down it contracts and holds the gold or silver in place without a trace of adhesive. The metal does not penetrate right through the shell and therefore is not seen on the reverse. As the metal is quite pure it takes a wonderful shine and produces dazzling little pinpricks of light. This technique is known as 'piqué point' or 'piqué d'or' and looks beautiful when in use, but if a fan decorated in this way is put in store, then the piqué-work and tortoiseshell can become dull and lacklustre. To cure that, you must rub in a little gun-oil (or fine machine oil) on the tip of the finger all over the shell and hold it in your hand until the shell is warm and the oil has evaporated, then buff up the piqué work.

During the eighteenth century some piqué decoration became more emphatic, with chased and detailed relief-work, and is named 'posé d'or'; the piqué d'or or piqué point (tiny nailhead work) was then often used as a background to the posé d'or. This is evident during the mid-eighteenth century, especially when you see minute chinoiserie motifs on tortoiseshell. Here the tortoiseshell has some embossing, so the shell was first softened by boiling in salted water so that patterns could be tool-impressed upon it, the motifs appearing in relief. Then the soft metal foil was laid on the embossments and cemented into position. Should a tortoiseshell stick or guard of the eighteenth century have to be cleaned, great care should be taken in case the embossed gold becomes loosened.

In England (as opposed to Germany and France) the gold-encrusted chinoiserie designs were not as popular; instead the English piqué workers developed what is known as the 'hair-line posé d'or', which meant they made their designs (landscapes or pictorial scenes) with lines of pure gold or pure silver, as delicate as pen drawing: the designs became more elaborate in the nineteenth century. Matthew Bolton of Birmingham was a pioneer in working with tortoiseshell in England, gradually incorporating forms of factory production which in no way destroyed the quality of the work. He made and sold lathes for delicate engine-turning as well, and in 1780 he acquired the business of the well-known tortoiseshell craftsman, John Gimblett. One natural result of the Birmingham and Sheffield factory trade in tortoiseshell was that the handcraftsman in piqué turned to ivory, and the loveliest gold stud work of piqué d'or was developed much more extensively than before on this almost equally inviting surface.

The French and the Germans developed the art of piqué work during the seventeenth and eighteenth centuries, especially in tortoiseshell. The Huguenots brought the technique to Britain after the Revocation of the Edict of Nantes, and the styles were treated more 'with the English restraint'. The Italians seemed more accomplished with early silver piqué-work in ivory, but the techniques quickly spread across Europe. During the nineteenth century piqué-work was extensively used on tortoiseshell for jewellery, especially in England after 1872, when a great deal was made by machine in Birmingham.

A third, 'poor man's' technique was that of cut steels piqué. Here the metal is cut steel, rather than a pure metal, the holes are larger, the background material (such as aromatic wood) does not expand, so a strong adhesive is required. It was widely used during the nine-teenth century, especially in fans made for Spain.

One method whereby one can determine whether animal products (such as ivory or tortoiseshell) are genuine, without laboratory testing, is that it is almost unknown for fan makers to use pure metals with cheap background materials, nor do they use cut steels with good animal products. Therefore, for instance, cut steels were used on horn but rarely on fine tortoiseshell; on bone instead of good ivory. Also piqué d'or would not have been used on plastics or bone.

Some silver or gold piqué-work can be slightly raised; almost all cut steels work is inlaid and flat: if there is a decorative nailhead cut steel work on a fan it is generally kept to the guards. All the piqué techniques were used to enrich a fan in some way and to reflect the novelties in new methods of lighting—from new forms of candles (and looking glasses) in the eighteenth century to gaslight in the nineteenth century. Illustration Nos. XX, XXXVII, XXXVIII, 12, 22.

PLASTIC FANS

Plastics, in the modern meaning of the word, are synthetic materials that are capable of being formed into usable products by heating, milling, moulding etc: the term is derived from the Greek 'plastikos', 'to form'.

The first plastic was Parkesine, later called Xylonite, exhibited by the English chemist and inventor Alexander Parkes in 1862. Celluloid was first seen in 1869, invented by John W. Hyatt. Bakelite was the first completely synthetic plastic, commercially produced in 1910 by Leo Hendrik Baekeland, a Belgian-born American chemist. After that we have to consider the use of polymers. Many fans had sticks made from plastics in the nineteenth century: they were not especially cheap at the beginning but they were certainly valued for their novelty. The material was tough, with great tensile strength, resistance to water, oils and dilute acids and eventually capable of low-cost production in a variety of colours. Fan sticks (many were small and/or brisé) could be made to look like amber, tortoiseshell, ivory ('ivorine'), etc., the 'give-away' factor being its own even-ness in colour and patterning. Plastics were extremely easily destroyed by fire. See page 59, *The Book of Fans*.

PORNOGRAPHIC FANS (see FOUR SCENES FANS)

PRICKED WORK ON FANS (see DECOUPÉ FANS)

PUNKAH

In Hindi the generic term for a fan is 'pankha', from 'pankh'—a feather

XVI. German fan, with a double silk leaf painted with a family in a park, a canary, a finch and flowers, trimmed with braid and sequins. Sticks of blonde turtleshell, carved and pierced, applied with silver and two colours of gold. Guards backed with mother-of-pearl. Opens 160 degrees. 11" : 28 cms. c 1775. Owned by Mrs Pamela Hudson.

XVII. Chinoiserie style fan (French), the leaf printed and painted with a cartoon lampooning the Chinese (the man on the left, selling grotesques and with a scroll notice 'Marchand de Magots') and the Europeans (the man with the Duke of Wellington's hat and smoking a meerschaum). 11½" : 29 cms. c 1830. Owned by Mrs Pamela Hudson.

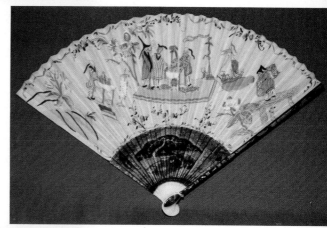

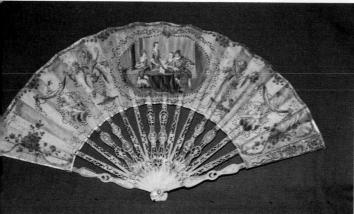

XVIII. Eighteenth century fan, probably French, the ivory satin leaf having an applied 'Teniers' scene surmounted by a heart, putti in the reserves. Oriental vases of flowers and the whole embellished with braid and spangles. The ivory sticks and guards are curved, pierced and overlaid with silver. c 1770. 11" : 28 cms. Owned by Mrs Pamela Hudson.

XIX. Combination fan. The sticks are of silvered ivory, carved putti and trophies, very finely crafted. c 1770. The leaf was applied c 1845, of silk, embroidered with sequins and a small painting. Obviously someone considered the sticks too good to throw away when the leaf became damaged, possibly with candle-grease. Owned by Mrs Pamela Hudson.

XX. *Horne fan, brisé, with piqué-point decoration.* c 1810–20. $6\frac{1}{4}''$: 16 cms. *Owned by Mrs Georgette Tilley.*

XXI. *Fontage fan, the leaf of printed silk, showing a swan, and signed A. T. Romasse; the sticks of blonde tortoiseshell, one guardstick marked 'Duvelleroy'. French.* $10\frac{1}{2}''$: 26.75 cms. c 1900. *Owned by Mrs Georgette Tilley.*

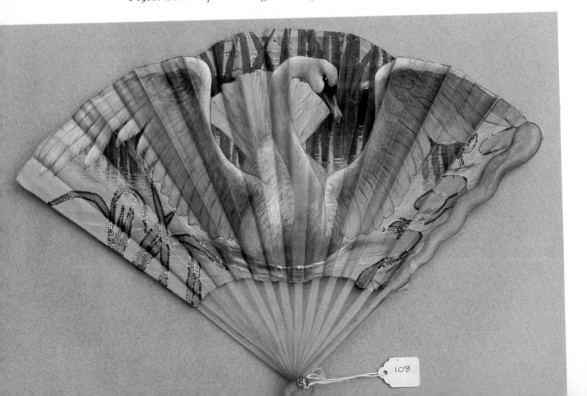

XXII. *Varnished fan, probably French. This is a brisé fan, of ivory sticks, the obverse painted with a scene of 'The Abduction of Helen' and then varnished. Erroneously called a 'Vernis Martin' fan in the past. $8\frac{1}{2}''$: 21.5 cms. c 1700. Private Collection.*

XXIII. *Directoire fan, brisé, of alternating ivory and sandalwood ; the central decoration is a coloured stipple engraving. $10\frac{1}{4}''$: 26 cms. c 1790. Private Collection.*

XXIV. Mother-of-pearl fan, the leaf
showing a painting of 'classical lovers', the
fine sticks, carved and gilt; has paintings
of 'palatial edifices' in the reserves.
$12\frac{1}{4}''$: 31.5 cms. c 1860. Private Collection.

XXV. Detail of same fan, showing one of
the 'palatial edifices' within gilt scrolls.

or bird's wing. The usage of this word is current in South-East Asia, which was strongly permeated with cultural and religious influences from the Indian sub-continent. On the whole people now feel the word refers to the large ceiling fans seen in the East, developed from the long flaglike ceiling fans of the past which were pulled by a rope.

PUZZLE FANS (see TRICK FANS)

QUIZZING FANS (see LORGNETTE FANS)

RESERVE (see CARTOUCHE)

REVERSED PAINTING FANS

This type were mainly made in the nineteenth century and chiefly in France. They were perfectly normal folding fans, generally of textile which was semi-transparent (such as a silk gauze), and they had a painted decoration (usually of gouache) of some scene where at least one person was seen 'face on' and another was seen with the back facing the viewer. On the reverse of the fan you saw exactly the same scene, but the person who was seen 'face on' was portrayed with his back to you, etc. The method was to attach an extra shaped piece of the textile on the reverse and paint upon that—but only over the area where the scene altered. There is one extant showing a gentleman leaning over a stone wall, speaking to a pretty lady: the reverse shows the other side of that wall, all of the gentleman, and only half of the lady because the wall obscures her. Another (Spanish) one shows on the obverse a gentleman of fashion with no less than three ladies on each arm. Reverse the fan and you see all their back views as they promenade. In some cases the fan is a straight reverse view painted onto a paper leaf (one is extant with back and front views of a scotty dog) and others are created from textiles with a double central section. The sticks and guards are made to complement the scene and many were made by Alexandre and Duvelleroy in Paris.

RIKIU OGI

The Japanese form of Tea Ceremony is accurately named *cha-no-yu*, and the fans used in these ceremonies are known as Rikiu ogi. The cult of the Tea Ceremony was a genuine instrument of culture with a lasting effect on the arts. Its allusive, restrained aesthetic is one of simplicity and elimination of the insignificant. Tea drinking, which originated in China, was first practised in Japan during the Kakamura period (1192–1333), by Zen monks trying to keep awake during meditation in their study halls. It later became an active part of Zen ritual and, in the fifteenth century, it came to mean a gathering of friends brought together in an isolated atmosphere to drink tea and discuss the aesthetic merits of painting, calligraphy and flower arrangements displayed in an alcove called the *toko-no-ma*, or quite often to discuss the merits of the tea utensils themselves. Fans were used at these ceremonies, not to fan oneself, but as plates on which to pass small cakes. These fans were composed of a very few sticks (three or four) and a simple leaf.

RIVETS

This is one of the most important parts of a fan as it holds it all together at the head. The rivet is self-explanatory: it is a piece of metal (sometimes known as a 'pin') round which pivot the sticks of both a brisé fan and a folding fan. Some of the early ones were known as 'barrel' rivets, in that they were composed of two pieces, one part screwing into another, often with a decorative tip such as a 'jewel' of paste. These have to be treated with immense care as they are made from a very thin metal and, after all these years, would easily split if one attempted to unscrew them. Later on the rivet turned into a simple piece of metal which was driven through the hole in the head and turned back upon itself. Very often there is a type of washer, or button (mother-of-pearl, tortoiseshell, etc.) which is added for strength and protection as well as decoration. In the nineteenth century a loop was added, attached to the rivet, through which ribbons might hang and be knotted. See also LOOPS, PARTS OF A FAN, and Chapter 5.

ROCOCO

This is a term in art describing a dainty and decorative style that originated chiefly in Paris in the early eighteenth century but was soon adopted throughout France and later in other countries, principally Germany and Austria. At the outset the style represented a reaction to the grand ponderousness of Louis XIV's Palais de Versailles and the official art of his reign. The noble and the wealthy bourgeoisie wished to reinstate Paris as the cultural centre of the country and built new residences, ordering them to be decorated in a lighter, more intimate style.

The proportions of the Rococo style are tall and slender. Mouldings are curved into 'C' scrolls, and asymmetry rather than symmetry is the rule. Light pastels, ivory-white and gold are the predominant colours and Rococo decorators made much use of mirrors. The decorative arts of the period *c* 1715 to 1745 admirably exemplified the Rococo tendencies, for it was a style better suited to them than to architecture.

Fans of the Rococo period are possibly the finest ever made in Europe, with their lightness of design, delicacy of carving, pastel shades (like the colours of the new porcelain) and foil-work within the guards to simulate the new mirrors. It is said that the word was made up from 'rocaille' and 'coquille' (pebbles and shells) because the style also featured elaborate stylised, shell-like, rock-like and scroll motifs, often in gold, gilt or gilded bronzes. Originally 'rocaille' was confined to the shellwork of artificial grottoes found in late-Renaissance gardens, but it broadened to mean more during the Rococo period.

Rococo fans exhibit fan making in its best period, when a leaf was 'married' to its sticks, all coming from the same 'stable' of craftsmen. They seem to be custom-made and the cleverest (and most expensive) show one scene painted upon the broad leaf and motifs from that scene painted or crafted into the sticks and guards. This is also the time when the sticks and guards were most wonderfully made, carved, pierced, engraved, embossed, repoussée, clouté and be-jewelled—and they are poems of decorative harmony.
Illustration Nos. XVI, XVIII, 8, 13, 14.

SANDALWOOD FANS
Fans have been made from sandalwood, which is the common name for semiparasitic plants of the genus Santalum and refers especially to the fragrant wood of the true, or white, sandalwood—*Santalum album*. Approximately 25 species of *Santalum* are distributed throughout south-eastern Asia and the islands of the South Pacific. Many other woods are used as substitutes for the true sandalwood, which grows to a height of about 33 feet (10 metres). Both tree and roots contain a yellow aromatic oil, called sandalwood oil, the odour of which persists for years in such articles as ornamental boxes, furniture and fans

made of the white sapwood. The oil is obtained by steam distillation of the wood and is used in perfumes, soaps, candles, incense, etc. Powdered sandalwood is used in the paste applied to make Brahmin caste marks and in sachets for scenting clothes. The wood itself is fine-grained and does not split when carved and pierced, which makes it perfect for creating fan sticks. It should not be confused with cedarwood, which is also aromatic but is red-tinged, decay-resistant and insect-repellant.

In the East, owners often dipped their sandalwood fans into a bowl of water to cool themselves down more efficiently, but they could not do this in the West as they generally decorated brisé sandalwood fans (they are all brisé) with engravings in a central cartouche (in the eighteenth and nineteenth centuries) or with cut steels piqué. They were mainly made in England and France and occasionally they were paired with a contrasting material such as ivory.

SCREEN FANS
For Oriental screen fans please see UCHIWA (for Japanese) or PIEN-MIEN (for Chinese). European screen fans will be found under HANDSCREENS.

SEQUINS AND SPANGLES
A sequin is always circular, a spangle is always shaped. The first known sequin was made in Venice: a gold coin there had been current (first minted in *c* 1280) named a zecchino, which was very small and circular. When, during the sixteenth century, these coins were suddenly withdrawn from usage, many people became extremely annoyed, especially one grand lady who had made a large collection of them 'for a rainy day'. In protest she had each of her coins pierced with a hole, sewed them all on to a spectacular dress and 'twinkled all over town'; she did not get the act rescinded but she did start a fashion in dress.

Spangles came along slightly later and, to differentiate between the two, the spangle came in a huge variety of shapes, leaving the sequin to its original coin shape. They were most popular during the eighteenth and nineteenth centuries. They did not always remain gold in colour but could also be silver, emerald green, red, blue, pink, etc. They were only used in the West, never in the Far East.

However, spangles and sequins are well-known in India and Pakistan: the maker of spangles was known as the *bindligar*, the word for

33. The black gauze leaf of this fan is decorated with the figure of an acrobat made from gold sequins, mounted on plain ebony sticks. French. 19th century. 9½″ : 24 cms. By courtesy of Bonhams, Knightsbridge.

spangle being *bindli*. They were cut out of thin sheets of fine gold or silver known as *sitta*, and then worked with a small anvil (*ahran*), scissors (*mikruz*), forceps (*chumti*), parchment (*chamra charmi*) and small pincers (*sanni*). Many fans from this sub-continent were also decorated with gold thread (*kalabutun*), thin tinsel (*sulma*), tinsel-wire (*mukesh*) and gold ribbon (*ghota, kinara*). The people enriched their garments with silks, cloth-of-gold and sumptuous velvets; their side-mounted flag and other shaped fans lent themselves to all forms of decoration, from embroidery to spangles and innumerable small discs of mirror-glass. Illustration Nos. XIX, XXIII, XXXI, XXXV, XXXVII, XL, 33.

SHADOW FANS FROM JAVA

These are rigid fans from Java, quite small, which were made of buffalo-hide for the main section, strengthened by supports and with a handle of carved buffalo-horn. On the surface of the hide would be painted their traditional Wayang shadow-puppets, often in solid col-

ours of red with gold, and sometimes stylised peacocks as well. They were made all over Indonesia, especially during the nineteenth and twentieth centuries. See also PARCHMENT.
Illustration No. XII.

SHAPED-FABRIC FANS

These were made as cheap brisé fans with a simple piece of fabric cut out in scallops to imitate feathers and backed by a simple wooden stick, held together by a thin cord or thick thread. They were fashionable in Europe in the early 1870s. Their use continued into the twentieth century, some with scalloped paper instead of textile. A catalogue of Sears, Roebuck & Company of 1902 quotes a price of 26 cents. It is said that Jenny Lind used a fan such as this when on tour in the United States and in that country these fans are known as 'Jenny Linds'.

SHELL-SHAPED FANS

These small European folding fans were made c 1890–1935. The shape is shell-like with a scalloped edge. One noted collector has one made of silver sequins on silver net, with mother-of-pearl sticks, in a perfect scallop-shell shape. They were decorated in the prevailing styles. See also FONTAGE FANS, PALMETTO FANS.

SLATE FANS

There are still some slate quarries in Wales where the apprentice is expected, as his 'Master's Piece', to make a fan from one thick slab of black slate. He would have to place a screw at one end, around which the sticks would doubly revolve. The slate would then be most minutely divided and sub-divided into equal sections, showing his skill as a worker, and then all the sticks would be pulled out equally and a double fan would emerge, the points of the outer guards arranged to touch the surface on which it stood. It is a remarkable exercise in both mathematics and the worker's skill as a slate-worker. These fans can still be bought at places like slate quarries in Wales and big agricultural fairs such as the Royal Bath and West Show.

SPANGLES (See SEQUINS)

STAMPED OR PUNCHED WORK ON FANS (See DECOUPÉ FANS)

STRAW

This is the residue remaining after cereals are threshed to remove the grains. It consists of dried stalks, leaves and husks of such grains and it was quite often used in Germany, France and possibly the Low Countries for decorating fans, some having first been dyed. Straw was only ever used in Europe as a form of decoration in very small reserves, rather than being a full type of fan, and often in conjunction with other applied materials, such as feathers, on silk or fine rag-paper. As the fan had to fold, only very small pieces of straw could be used, often less than $\frac{3}{4}''$ (2 cm) long, or there would have been a risk of splitting or flaking, but longer pieces are known to have been laid lengthwise along a pleat. Some of the prettiest 'straw' fans show a tiny birdcage made of only eight pieces of very fine straw, with an even tinier bird inside, made of applied feathers. So fine is this work that the owner of such a fan may mistake the decoration for embroidery. See also VEGETABLE FIBRES FOR FANS.
Illustration No. 34.

34. The English version of the Chinese Applied Faces fan, pre-dating their great vogue. The vellum leaf is painted in watercolours showing three figures all with clothes of silk applied onto the leaf and faces of applied ivory; also in the decoration is straw, and stamped-paper flowers. In the centre is a hand-coloured aquatint of 'The Arts' after Angelica Kaufmann. The sticks are of carved and pierced ivory with blue and white Staffordshire ceramic medallions set in the guards. c 1790–1800. Private Collection.

SUEHIRO

One author spells this word 'Suehiro' and another spells it 'Suyehiro':
one never knows whether to follow the discipline of an academic or
the everyday experience of an author/collector in these matters . . .
let us hope it does not signify. The word is Japanese and means 'wide-
ended'—a new type of fan for the Japanese after they had first seen
fans from China which had a double leaf—the Japanese traditionally
only used one. These new double leaves were introduced during the
Muromachi period (1392–1568) and, in order to deal with the problem
of a thicker leaf, the guards were designed to bend outwards from
the middle. This means that when the fan is closed the leaf section
looks as if it is half-open, even though the lower sticks are firmly shut.

TEA CEREMONY FANS (See RIKIU OGI)

TELESCOPIC FANS

Another word could be 'expanding'; it is quite extraordinary how
often a new owner is slightly puzzled to own a thick, squat fan and
is unaware that it pulls out to a 'proper' shape. This type appears perfectly normal as a folding fan but with short, stocky, straight sticks
and guards. However, if the mount is gently pulled away from the
gorge area when the fan is closed, the sticks seem to expand to twice
their length: when the fan is opened out again it still appears the same
fan but with the sticks twice as long and half as thick. The reason for
this was entirely practical and novel: to save space. During the eighteenth century many telescopic fans were made of paper and during
the nineteenth they were made from textiles. There are always exceptions to this rule, and there were also other types of telescopic fan which
had sticks jointed in two sections.
Illustration Nos. I, II, III.

TOPOGRAPHICAL FANS

It is said that topographical fans, especially English examples, are rare.
Topography is the collective term for all the physical features of an
area, and in fans it generally includes figures as well. As an example,
there is an illustration on page 69 of *A Collector's History of Fans* which
shows a scene whose caption, at the time of publication, was vague
and eventually found to be totally incorrect. Following help from the

35. Topographical fan, the chicken-skin leaf painted with a trompe l'oeil of three Italian views, La Grotta de Pozzuoli duputazione de la salute di Napoli *and also* La Grotta del Cana *: the bone sticks pierced and the guards carved with figures and foliage. Italian.* $11\frac{1}{2}''$ *: 29 cms. (Fetched £150 in November 1982.) By courtesy of Christies, South Kensington.*

Royal Institute of British Architects (initiated by Anthony Vaughan) the fan has now been identified as being by Thomas Robins, showing Ralph Allen of Bath, together with John Wood the Elder, examining huge building blocks of Bath stone which were destined for Prior Park, Ralph Allen's 'country' house (on the hill just outside the City), lying ready in Ralph Allen's Stone Mason's Yard. The buildings in the background are now found to have been built for the stone masons and wharf-workers, the first 'real' commission of John Wood the Elder, and the River Avon lies on the right. It has taken much time to discover all these facts and, much to my delight and by pure coincidence, two years ago, I managed to buy the first of these cottages (on the left of the painting) for myself. They were built in 1727 and were due to be knocked down for road-widening some years ago, but fortunately the conservationists of Bath fought tooth and nail to keep them. Illustration No. 35.

TORTOISESHELL

The tortoise is a land-dwelling turtle, while turtles are aquatic or semi-aquatic creatures. Although tortoiseshell used for decorative purposes is really the shell taken from the hawk's-bill turtle (*Eretmochelys imbricata*), other forms of tortoiseshell are taken from other types of tortoise and turtle, and the use of the word 'tortoiseshell' (although not always completely accurate) is better understood than 'turtle shell'.

The marbled, varicoloured pattern and deep translucence of the plates (shells) of the creature have long been valued. Tortoiseshell was imported to Rome from Egypt, and in seventeenth century France the work attained a high level of artistry.

Basically, the turtle is a reptile which has not changed its appearance since the Triassic Period. It is toothless, generally slow moving and completely unaggressive—which makes it all the more unsavoury to learn that turtles' shells (plates) are ripped from their bodies whilst they are still alive in order to keep the translucency (I have watched this being done in Sri Lanka). Just recently a new technique has been developed so that the animal may be killed humanely first (in the past the shell went opaque after the animal was dead) and this technique has

36. French fan, the leaf painted with three groups of elegant figures in a park, with five circular portrait miniatures suspended at intervals around the border, four of an elegant couple and their children, and one of a European dressed as a tartar; the tortoiseshell sticks carved with putti, pierced, painted with vignettes, silver and gilt, the guardsticks set with painted mother-of-pearl plaques. 10″ : 25.5 cms. c 1760. (Fetched £520 in July 1982.) By courtesy of Christies, South Kensington.

coincided with new conservation laws which forbid the importation of tortoiseshell into some countries (notably Britain). The shell is light, strong, easily worked and most attractive and rich-looking. It was used for both sticks and guards and sometimes as both an inlay in other materials and as a strengthener by the head of a fan. Imitation tortoiseshell was used also: one type was made from stained horn and another was a dyed plastic. It was effectively used with piqué-work. Illustration Nos. XVI, XXI, 27, 36, 47.

TRICK FANS

In order to startle your companions, a certain type of fan was made whereby you picked it up (or you invited them to do so) and it appeared to fall into nine broken pieces. After the initial cries of horror and shock you then picked it up yourself and it immediately appeared 'mended'. The 'trick' is the method by which the fan is either ribboned or mounted, and this is highly elaborate. Some are made all of ribbons, others of ribbons and lace alternately, and some are brisé. Conjurors used these in the last quarter of the nineteenth century but, because

37 a&b Trick fan, the ribbons of chine silk with flowers, the sticks being of decorated bone. The owner opens it up one way and it appears perfectly normal, opened the other way it falls apart into sections. Almost all fans only open from left to right apart from the Four Scenes fans, a few dance fans and this third category of Trick fans. Late 19th century c., English, 10" : 25.5 cms. Owned by Mrs Georgette Tilley.

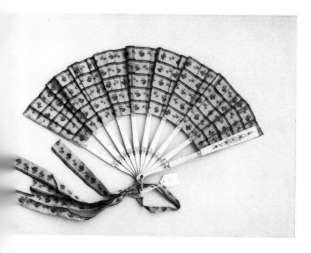

they had to be seen from the stage, they were enormous in size. Everything depends on whether you open the fan up from left to right or right to left and, on careful examination, you will find that the sticks are arranged in pairs and the ribboning highly complicated. Illustration No. 37.

T'UAN-SHAN

This is the Chinese name for a ceremonial fan. It was a screen fan but larger and mounted on a long handle. It was initially used in the ceremonial entourage of high officials (according to Julia Hutt) and, subsequently, at any important function or procession, together with the ceremonial umbrella and banner. Julia Hutt goes on to say (in *Fans from the East*) that the distinction between the ceremonial fan and banner is a difficult one to make for they often served a dual purpose. They go back for centuries.

UCHIWA

This Japanese word means a rigid screen fan: these could be mounted or left as a painting. As early as 930 there was a Japanese dictionary which listed both the 'ogi' (folding fan) and the 'uchiwa' (screen fan).

VARNISHED FANS

The general overall term is often 'Vernis Martin' but since the production of Hans Huth's book *Lacquer in the West: the History of a Craft and an Industry 1550–1950* and the author's own full chapter on 'Western European Varnished or Japanned Fans' in *The Book of Fans*, it seems agreed by collectors that the term 'varnished' is the most accurate. However, old habits die hard; auction houses set out to please the collectors and so keep to the old term of 'Vernis Martin', so we must consider them all together.

These fans were made in Holland, England and France *c* 1650–*c* 1730 and then again in the nineteenth century in admiration of past styles and techniques. Some were painted onto imported Chinese ivory sticks, very small and wedge-shaped and which, in the 1720s, became known as 'Lilliputians'. Some were created from scratch on tiny ivory brisé fans, wedge-shaped and keeping the Chinese style of having a 'different' decoration on guards and gorge. The date most associated with this type of fan is *c* 1700 (some were made as early as *c* 1680, some up to 1730), and these fans are rare. A great deal more research is needed on these fans, especially as they are immensely expensive and, since by now the paint and varnish tends to flick off when handled, they are becoming very delicate.

They were painted on prepared ivory with oil paints and then coated with a varnish to protect the paint; it should be mentioned that on no account should these fans be cleaned ... the decoration merely washes off. The subjects most seen are either theatrical or mythological, or from the classics of Racine and Corneille. Some of the fans then display a mirror image on the reverse, which came from working in the Chinese manner of placing the fan upon a thin sheet of glass and positioning a candle underneath; the artist could then trace the design. Sometimes only the outline of the design is done and sometimes there is a complete repainting of the scene.

To hold the fan together there is either a tough, thin cord or knots of fine silk, or a fine silk ribbon about $\frac{3}{4}''$ (2 cm) wide. This ribbon is also known to have been made of fine skin. The ribbon is then hand-painted (not woven) with a design. Sometimes the design is in minia-ture, differing for every pleat; sometimes it is geometric; often it is of delicate gold lines.

On other fans of this type the reverse painting can be just as ac-complished as the obverse but exhibiting either a landscape or a seas-cape. One noted collector feels that the way one can tell that a fan was made in France is to look for a wide cartouche in which there is a painting, irregular in shape, with heavy gilding on its outline and with some pierced work through the surrounding ivory leaves. Other-wise one can only rely upon one's knowledge of the prevailing styles of painting in various countries for a fan's place of manufacture.

It is also of interest to examine the manufacture of these fans: some, if taken apart for some reason, show that they numbered the sticks as they numbered good furniture parts. On others you can see how the artist would paint each stick in such a way that, when the fan was held up and opened, the scene did not abruptly stop at the edge of each stick but was painted a certain amount across, underlying the over-lapping leaf. These fans appear to be of northern European manufacture and show deep tones of colour.

Illustration Nos. XIV, XXII.

VEGETABLE FIBRES FOR FANS

Fans, especially ethnographical ones, have been made from a variety of vegetable fibres all over the world from the beginning of time. They have also been made from reeds, *dib*; dry flags, *Typha angustifolia*; bagar grass, *Eriophorum cannabinum*; the inner bark of the dhaman (*Grewia oppositifolia*), *Fothergilla involucrata*; nettle-bark tree (*Celtis*), *Crotolaria, Saccharum officinaram*—and a huge variety of palms. Some of these materials are plaited, some woven, and some treated in the style of Indian 'chicks', a form of meshed bamboo for screening windows and verandahs. Many have been dyed, or have dyed fibres interwoven which make up some form of patterning. They are, on the whole, cheap local crafts which cost nothing (except time) to make.
Illustration No. 38.

VERNIS MARTIN (See VARNISHED FANS, LILLIPUTIAN FANS)

VIGNETTE (See CARTOUCHE)

WEDDING FANS (See MARRIAGE FANS)

ZŌGE OGI

During the mid-nineteenth century the Japanese made some very fine ivory brisé fans which were completely different from the ivory brisé fans of China. The Chinese pierced and carved the ivory, the Japanese applied both gold and semi-precious stones on to the ivory—exactly the opposite in technique. The Chinese divided the whole fan into three separate sections (above the ribbon, below the ribbon, and the gorge area) whereas the Japanese treated the fan as a complete canvas. They used rather thick ivory sticks and even thicker ivory guards, all with shaped finials (never the wedge-shape you see in some Chinese ivory brisé fans) and then created some exquisite scenes in *takamaki-e* or *hira-maki-e*, complicated layers of gold and lacquer which take a very long time to complete to such sophistication. On occasion the guard is similarly decorated and becomes a continuation of the scene; on other occasions shibayama inlay is used in another design (tiny insects, flowers and so on of jade, coral, or mother-of-pearl). These fans appear to have been made only from *c* 1860–*c* 1890 and some are signed.
Illustration No. XXXIV.

38. *Australian fans. Top left: a woven fan made by aboriginal women from Elcho Island, off the Northern Territory, taught by Fijian missionaries. Centre top: a fly-whisk made by aboriginals of emu feathers stuck onto a stick with native beeswax. Top right: woven fan made by aboriginals at the Mapoon mission station (now closed). Centre bottom: brisé fan made of Queensland woods by servicemen during the 1939-45 war in North Queensland. Owned by Mrs Audrey North.*

4 Identifying Illustrative Techniques

DRESS IN PORTRAITURE

Man's physical appearance throughout pictorial history, if recorded by a professional (artist in the past, photographer today), has always been a deliberate statement.

Details have always been accurately recorded, but the essence behind the presentation has generally been more of an oblique lie, because this recording might have been a 'once-in-a-lifetime' event. Even today, when a professional photographer is brought in to record an event of note, men and women still appear in 'fancy dress'.

No baby wears a lace christening gown more than once, any more than a bride would wear her wedding gown to a supermarket—yet posterity may only see us in these special clothes. The cheap but realistic home snapshot is now an honest assessment of our clothes and surroundings but is only a phenomenon of the twentieth century; if one is going to the expense of engaging a professional artist or photographer, one naturally wants to end up with something extra-special . . . and so it has been for the past 500 years. We should therefore look at paintings of the past (including, in miniature, on fans) with a carefully discerning eye.

The monarchs and courts of the sixteenth century were widely painted but portraits of the bourgeoisie were rare. This was partly because of the expense and partly because of a completely different critical attitude towards portraiture and dress at that time, which continued for several centuries.

Why was a portrait painted at all? To record a special event. When recording this event, how much could legitimately be the truth and how much was manipulated as a public relations exercise? A classic example was the vast painting of the Coronation of Napoleon, which included quite a few people who were not present on the day, left out some incidents and showed others that never occurred.

Paintings were propaganda, and an artist worked from an extremely carefully drawn up contract which specified every detail, from how many people should be portrayed, to the exact positioning of a family jewel, and how many colours were to be employed. Paintings were 'modern', showing both society's newest attitudes and the family's latest acquisitions, but they were also planned to last and not 'date'. This convention continued until mid-Victorian times; so, when examining a painted fan, one should heed the prevailing tastes in painting as a whole when attempting to date it and not go by clothes alone.

A number of later Elizabethan and early Jacobean paintings have survived in which the sitters are depicted wearing dress markedly different from their normal fashionable clothes. Their 'strange fantastick habit' would have been worn at a masque, an entertainment which had been introduced from Italy into the court of Henry VIII and had become a very popular feature of Elizabethan court life. Design of masque dress was governed by certain conventions, the most important being that it should not resemble 'examples of known attires' (Francis Bacon, *Of Masques and Triumphs*, 1597), an attitude which persisted for many years afterwards. This search for exotic costume led the designer to consult illustrations of the national dress of faraway countries, a fairly easy task as many costume books were published in the latter half of the century; by 1600 it is apparent from visual and documentary evidence that the garments worn at the English masque were influenced by Renaissance theatre costume.

Certain types of historical costume, mainly sixteenth and seventeenth century, appear frequently in eighteenth-century English and French portraiture, reflecting not only a nostalgia for the idealised past, but also the popularity of such costumes as worn at masquerades. When seen on painted fan-leaves this tends to confuse the new collector and shows how important it is to consider the entire fan with its sticks, guards and rivet, when attempting to date it. I have a fan, for instance, where all the gentlemen are dressed in Roman armour, the ladies in 'nightdresses' and the central lady in a fashionable dress of the 1730s, together with the contemporary jewels: all the other details date the fan to c 1740.

Seventeenth century Baroque artists were so worried about their pictures looking out of date (because of the costume becoming dated) that they tried to find clothes that would not date. They first tried

39. The leaf of this fan is painted with the 'Departure of a Hero', after a picture by a follower of De Troy signed Parmentier, the mother-of-pearl sticks carved with shepherds and shepherdesses, pierced, gilt and backed with mother-of-pearl. $11\frac{1}{4}$″ : 28.5 cms. c 1880. (Fetched £180 in March 1982.) By courtesy of Christies, South Kensington.

the 'Arcadian' vogue, as can be seen in the works of Van Dyck and Rembrandt, but this, too, was a fashion, so another form was sought.

The middle of the seventeenth century promoted the 'Roman look', as it was an unchanged type of clothing which they thought would last. Van Dyck, Lely, and many others used it, but were not aware that the style dated as much as the wigs and pearls the sitters wore. That brings us to status: no matter how dateless the picture was meant to be, the sitters were not prepared to leave out those signals of their rank, the wigs, jewels and lace, which their contemporaries understood. For men the 'Roman costume' was mainly armour, but a way had to be found to paint non-military people, like writers and ladies. The answer was to use undress, either Indian gowns or shifts with a fabric over them (such as my fan with the 'nightdresses'). This was shocking, to show people in undress in public, but it was another form of status, for those at the top of society can ignore the rules and get away with it, while the lower orders cannot. Undress was allowed in court art, but was not approved by the Protestant middle class. Hence my fan must have been painted for a lady at court to use, since no lady down the social scale would have displayed it, for fear (and very genuine at that) of the disapproval of her contemporaries.

During the eighteenth century there was a growing appreciation of the glories of English history during the Tudor and Stuart periods and a gradual development of accuracy in historical costume on the stage and as used by the painter of history. The years 1730–1789 showed a lack of moderation in painting with an exaggerated cult of the aristocracy and of the military, both ladies and gentlemen using make-up to contrast with the vogue for powdered hair. During the Rococo period fashions spread quickly over the whole of Europe. The French ideas penetrated even into such artistically independent places as Venice, Rome, Vienna and Berlin, so that everywhere the salons and their frequenters were identical in appearance—for the first time paintings became truly international in depicting the sitter and fashions in dress.

The year 1792 in France (with the fall of the monarchy and the establishment of a people's commune) marked a decisive date in the evolution of costume for men. Jacques-Louis David, the leading painter of his day, was invited to present his ideas for official costumes for men in order to distinguish people in authority (they were not adopted), and the best proof that contemporaries themselves saw a connection between official dress and political outlook is furnished by a delightful little work entitled *Caricatures Politiques*, by Beauvart, dated 1798. It is important, therefore, to remember to look at the clothes a *man* wore at this time on European fan leaves, and to note also that 1792 is a fairly reliable cut-off point for French fans.

During the Empire period (c 1804–14) Napoleon was in charge of official dress. He possessed a real flair for its psychological import and instructed artists in the way he wanted himself and his court to be represented.

In Britain between 1820–1850, there was a great interest in national history, and public imagination was particularly captured by historical costume through which the past could come alive in a unique way. Many articles on costume history appeared in popular women's magazines—even in *Punch*—and the favourite form of activity in some circles was a 'fancy dress ball'. Some new collectors feel that early nineteenth-century fans are fakes because they show scenes of former centuries, but this is completely wrong: they did not try to fake earlier styles, or even techniques; they were attempting to show how learned they were in accurately representing the past. It is easy enough to see the difference; two guidelines are that powdered hair in nineteenth-century scenes is shown as white, whereas in the eighteenth century it would have been grey, and gilding is quite different and far more brassy.

During the nineteenth century, as many middle-class values took a downward trend, all the social classes began to participate in the public display of grief. Nineteenth century mourning dress is, in part, a manifestation of the new standards of respectability to which the middle classes laid claim — revelling in 'the luxury of woe'.

Black clothing was not, however, confined to mourning during this century; it was also the colour associated with the church, the business world of men and domestic service for women. It appealed to artists and poets of a romantic persuasion; it was flattering to a fair skin; it gave the illusion of slimness; it was dramatic as a contrast or foil to other colours and, not least, it was a practical choice for daily wear in polluted cities. All these uses of black can make distinguishing clothing problematic, especially for mourning. Relatives and friends were mourned in descending order and with a different shade and grade appropriate to each category, with much conflicting advice being poured out to their readers by women's magazines. As Henry Mayhew commented in 1865, 'our grief goes for nothing if not fashionable'. The fan collector must therefore beware of labelling a fan depicting ladies and gentlemen wearing black clothing as 'a mourning fan', for it may be nothing of the sort.

Not until the late nineteenth century did pictures of real peasants in working dress become popular, especially painted by the French and the Americans, but by that time owners of fine fans usually preferred satin, silks or feathers and not reproductions of contemporary art.

In general, therefore, European painted fans of the seventeenth, eighteenth and nineteenth centuries very often showed people in what we would consider 'fancy dress', and it is a *detail* rather than the costume which might give a clue to date. Not only do we owe a debt to art historians but also to costume historians: from David, Grasset de Saint Saveur, J. R. Planché and F. W. Fairholt in the past, to the famous

116

academics of today.

Illustrations on fans have been executed in a large variety of media, some of which it may be helpful to explain.

WATERCOLOURS

Watercolours are pigments ground with gum arabic and thinned with water in use. Sable and squirrel ('camel') hair brushes are used on white and tinted paper. In the 'pure' technique, often referred to as 'the English method', no white or other opaque pigment is applied, colour intensity and tonal depth being built up by successive, transparent washes on damp paper. Patches of white paper are left unpainted to represent white objects and to create effects of reflected light. These flecks of bare paper produce the sparkle characteristic of 'pure' watercolour. Tonal gradations and soft, atmospheric qualities are rendered by staining the paper when it is very wet with varying proportions of pigment. Sharp accents, lines and coarse textures are introduced when the paper has dried. Some fans have been coloured by watercolour paints, but you find no opacity in the colouring and, because of the

40. Italian fan, the parchment leaf finely painted with fisherfolk in a landscape, mounted on pierced and carved ivory sticks. First quarter of the 18th century. 11″ : 28 cms. By courtesy of Bonhams, Knightsbridge.

nature of various pigments, the paint sometimes tends to flake in tiny shards. Printed fans which were hand-tinted had watercolours used on them.

GOUACHE

Gouache is opaque watercolour. It is thinned with water for applying, with sable and hog-hair brushes, to white or tinted paper, card, or silk. Honey or starch is sometimes added to retard its quick-drying property. Liquid glue is preferred as a thinner by painters wishing to retain the tonality of colours (which otherwise dry slightly lighter in key) and to prevent thick paint from flaking. Gouache paints have the advantage that they dry out almost immediately to a matt finish and, if required, without visible brushmarks. These qualities, combined with a wide colour range and the capacity to be washed thinly or applied in thick impasto, make the medium particularly suitable for painting on fabrics. It is the medium that produces the suede finish and crisp lines characteristic of many Indian and Islamic miniatures, as well as Western screen and fan decoration. Because of its elasticity, the colour does not flake from a fan which is continually being folded and unfolded. Creamy gouache shades were used on all fan surfaces, including parchment (vellum, chicken skin), paper and textiles.

INKS

Ink is the traditional painting medium of China and Japan, where it has been used with long-haired brushes of wolf, goat or badger on silk or absorbent paper. Oriental black ink is a gum-bound carbon stick that is ground on rough stone and mixed with varying amounts of water to create a wide range of modulated tones, or applied almost dry, with lightly brushed strokes, to produce coarser textures. The calligraphic brush technique is expressive of Zen Buddhist and Confucian philosophies, brushstroke formulas for the spiritual interpretation of nature in painting dictating the use of the lifted brush tip for the 'bone', or 'lean', structure of things, and the spreading belly of the hairs for their 'flesh', or 'fat', volumes. The Far Eastern artist poises the brush vertically above the paper and controls its rhythmic movements from the shoulder. Distant forms represented in landscapes painted on silk were sometimes brushed on from the reverse side in order to create a mysterious illusion of depth. Oriental fans very often featured inks on both paper and textile surfaces, sometimes alone and sometimes with added colours.

IVORY PAINTING
Ivory painting was practised in the eighteenth and nineteenth centuries in Europe and America for portrait miniatures or for fans. The decoration was often oval in form, especially if a professional artist or miniaturist was asked to decorate a fan. They were painted under a magnifying glass in fairly dry water colours or tempera stippling, with sable or marten-hair brushes; corrections were made with a needle. The velvet quality of the colours was enhanced, on the thinner ivories, by the glow produced by gold-leaf or a tinted backing.

TEMPERA
A tempera medium is dry pigment tempered with an emulsion and thinned with water. True tempera (one of the most ancient of painting techniques) is made by mixing the pigment with the yolk of fresh eggs, although a manuscript illuminator often used egg white and some easel painters used the whole egg. This egg tempera is the most durable form of the medium, being generally unaffected by humidity and temperature. It dries quickly to form a tough film that acts as a protective skin to the support. In handling, in its diversity of transparent and opaque effects, and in the satin sheen of its finish, it resembles the modern acrylic emulsion paints. When seen on an ivory fan you can enjoy the satin sheen if you tip the fan from side to side to catch the light.

PRINTING
Printing has traditionally been defined as a technique for applying under pressure a certain quantity of colouring agent onto a specified surface to form a body of text or an illustration. By the end of the second century the Chinese had apparently discovered, empirically, a means of printing texts; certainly they then had at their disposal the three elements necessary for printing: (1) paper, the technique for the manufacture of which they had known for several decades; (2) ink, whose basic formula they had known for 25 centuries; and (3) surfaces bearing texts carved in relief.

Paper, the production of which was known only to the Chinese,

41. *Printed fan, the paper leaf decorated with hand-coloured satirical prints and slogans after the French Revolution of 1789; the reverse with the words of the song 'Le Trompe de L'Abbé Maury'; on wooden sticks. French. c 1790. 12½" : 31.5 cms. By courtesy of Bonhams, Knightsbridge.*

followed the caravan routes of Central Asia to the markets of Samarkand, whence it was distributed as a commodity across the entire Arab world. The transmission of the techniques of paper-making appears to have followed the same route: Chinese taken prisoner at the Battle of Talas, near Samarkand, in 751, gave the secret to the Arabs. Paper mills proliferated from the end of the eighth century to the thirteenth, from Baghdad and on to Spain, then under Arab domination. Paper first penetrated Europe as a commodity from the twelfth century onward, through Italian ports that had active relations with the Arab world and also, doubtless, by the overland route from Spain to France; quite possibly fans were brought over at the same time.

Paper-making techniques were apparently rediscovered by Europeans through an examination of the material from which the imported commodity was made; possibly the secret was brought back in the mid-thirteenth century by returning crusaders or merchants on the Eastern trade routes. Paper-making centres grew up in Italy after 1275 and in France and Germany in the course of the fourteenth century. Thus the essential elements of the printing process collected slowly in Western Europe, where a favourable cultural and economic climate had formed.

Wood-block printing began in the sixth century in China and movable type was invented about 1041–48 by a Chinese alchemist named Pi Sheng. Xylography, the art of printing from wood carving, appeared in Europe no earlier than the last quarter of the fourteenth century, spontaneously and presumably as a result of the use of paper. Metallographic printing appears to have been practised in Holland around 1430, while Gutenberg's invention of typography (the concept of the printing press itself had never been conceived in the Far East) is generally credited with the date c 1450, and the first all-metal press was constructed in England in about 1795—from then on the techniques fairly galloped ahead.

Before the invention of photography, prints were the only means of conveying visual information to people in quantity. It is important to note, however, that the information conveyed by prints is not necessarily accurate. Sometimes this is due to the process of printmaking itself. With most engravings, for example, the engraver and the artist were different people. The artist might go to a certain place (Venice, for instance) and sketch on the spot; later he 'worked up' that sketch to make it more picturesque. Then the drawing went to the engraver, where it might be re-drawn by an intermediary to the size of the plate on which it was to be engraved in reverse. Eventually proofs were taken and the plate amended as required; unless the artist was there to check everything, the end result might be almost unrecognisable.

With etching and lithography this was less likely to happen as in these techniques the artist was often responsible for the work on the plate or stone.

In Europe during the seventeenth and eighteenth centuries, most prints carried all the relevant information on their margins. There was no legal obligation for a publisher to copyright a design for a fan, for instance, but many did and, as long as there is one remaining fan leaf (mounted or not) with all the relevant information on it, all other fans from that date can be correctly dated. Below is a short list of some of the abbreviations commonly found on prints:

Del, delt, delin = drew (from *delineavit*).
Descripsit = drew.
Desig, designavit = designed.
Inv, invenit = designed.

Pinx, pinxit, ping, pingebat = painted.
(The above words are usually bottom left, referring to the original artist or draughtsman.)
Aqua, aquaforti = etched.
Aquatinta = engraved in aquatint by.
F, fecit, fac, faciebat = made by.
Imp (impresset) = he printed it.
Inc, incidit, incidebat = engraved.
Lith, lithog = lithographed by.
Sc, sculp, sculpsit, sculpebat = engraved.

It was William Hogarth who was mainly instrumental in bringing about the English Copyright Act of 1735, which made the copying of prints illegal for a period of 14 years after issue and ensured that the original artist and printmaker were not robbed of their profits—as had happened to Hogarth himself with *The Harlot's Progress*, published in 1732 and copied wholesale.

Some fan leaves have been decorated with woodcuts, hand-coloured: they are early and crude. A great many are *line-engraved*: this means a burin or graver pushed across the surface of a copper plate. This technique virtually came to an end about 1821; after 1850 the copper was coated with a thin layer of steel which, if it ever wore out, could be replaced. How can one tell the difference between the two techniques? With copper, the design looks 'heavier' and the parallel lines are spaced further apart; *steel engravings* have a lighter, 'silvery' feel, and the parallel and cross-hatched lines are fine and close together.

With *aquatints* the outline of the design is usually etched onto the plate at the start. This technique was developed in England in the 1770s, notably by Paul Sandby; the effect was designed to produce tonal variations, the finished prints resembling wash drawings or water colours. *Aquatints* could be printed in one- or two-coloured inks with further colours added by hand.

Mezzotints were developed in the mid-seventeenth century, became an English speciality and towards the end of the eighteenth century were used for animal studies and prints after the paintings of George Morland.

Stipple engraving is created by a pointed instrument being used to build up the image by dotting the etching ground. It was popular in

Britain in the late eighteenth century and there are many fans known to have been stipple engraved by Francesco Bartolozzi.

Lithography was discovered as a technique in 1798 and marked the first important development in printmaking in several centuries. It was invented by Alois Senefelder of Munich, but not much used in Britain until Charles Joseph Hullmandel set up his lithographic printing press in London in 1818. It soon overtook aquatint for topographical illustration but attracted commercial printers rather than artists of note. In 1851 the Post Office listed some 135 lithographic printers in London.

Printing was an ideal technique for some fans, especially when they became cheap and topical. The saying 'Off with the old, on with the new' applied very much to the stripping off of passé printed fan-leaves and the application of new ones. The greatest collector of printed fans and fan-leaves was Lady Charlotte Schrieber whose collection was given to the British Museum in 1891; the catalogue by Lionel Cust (which may often be seen in good libraries) is used as a yardstick by collectors, and is referred to by auction houses in sales catalogues.

THE LANGUAGE OF FANS

One may look at a pretty fan and one may also look at the pretty girl who owns that fan—and carry on an animated conversation with her when, to comply with convention, no real speech is permitted.

42. An embossed paper leaf fan decorated with a coloured lithograph, mounted on pierced and painted wooden sticks. Made for the Spanish market or actually in Spain. c 1860. 10½" : 26.5 cms. By courtesy of Bonhams, Knightsbridge.

In the past there have been several ways of using the fan for silent conversations; the first real satire on the way that ladies behaved behind their fans was published in *The Spectator* of 1711, when Joseph Addison (1672–1719) wrote a splendid essay describing a mythical academy for the training of young ladies and gentlemen in 'The Excerciſe of the Fan'.

In 1740 there was a reference to a conversation fan in *The Gentleman's Magazine* and, to avoid mistakes, I shall quote Wooliscroft Rhead (page 253, *History of the Fan*):

> Five signals are given, corresponding to the five divisions of the alphabet, the different letters, omitting the 'J', being capable of division into five, the movements 1 2 3 4 5 corresponding to each letter in each division. 1 By moving the fan with the left hand to right arm. 2 The same movement but with right hand to left arm. 3 Placing against bosom. 4 Raising it to the mouth. 5 To forehead.
>
> Example—Suppose *Dear* to be the word to be expressed. 'D' belongs to the first division, the fan must be moved to the right: then, as the number underwritten is 4, the fan is raised to the mouth. 'E' belonging to the same division, the fan is likewise moved to the right, and, as the number underwritten is 5, the fan is lifted to the head, and so forth. The termination of the word is distinguished by a full display of the fan, and as the whole directions with illustrations are displayed on the fan, this language is more simple than at first might appear.

It seems generally accepted that the first person to organise a 'language of the fan' was a Spaniard by the name of Fenella, who published (in Spanish) fifty directions on how to converse with the fan. Later on it was translated into German by Frau Bartholomaus and, finally, Duvelleroy of Paris translated it into English and made it available on small cards. The directions are refined into 33 actions and they 'speak' for themselves:

> Carrying in right hand in front of face: *Follow me*
> Carrying in left hand in front of face: *Desirous of acquaintance*
> Placing it on left ear: *I wish to get rid of you*
> Drawing across the forehead: *You have changed*

Twirling in the left hand: *We are watched*
Carrying in the right hand: *You are too willing*
Drawing through the hand: *I hate you*
Twirling in the right hand: *I love another*
Drawing across the cheek: *I love you*
Presented shut: *Do you love me?*
Drawing across the eyes: *I am sorry*
Touching tip with finger: *I wish to speak to you*
Letting it rest on right cheek: *Yes*
Letting it rest on left cheek: *No*
Open and shut: *You are cruel*
Dropping it: *We will be friends*
Fanning slowly: *I am married*
Fanning quickly: *I am engaged*
With handle to lips: *Kiss me*
Open wide: *Wait for me*
Carrying in left hand, open: *Come and talk to me*
Placed behind head: *Don't forget me*
With little finger extended: *Good-bye*
The shut fan held to the heart: *You have won my love*
The shut fan resting on the right eye: *When may I be allowed to see you?*
Presenting a number of sticks, fan part opened: *At what hour?*
Touching the unfolded fan in the act of waving: *I long always to be near thee*
Threaten with the shut fan: *Do not be so imprudent*
Gazing pensively at the shut fan: *Why do you misunderstand me?*
Pressing the half-opened fan to the lips: *You may kiss me*
Clasping the hands under the open fan: *Forgive me I pray you*
Cover the left ear with the open fan: *Do not betray our secret*
Shut the fully opened fan very slowly: *I promise to marry you*

During the nineteenth century the 'language of the fan' appears to have been enthusiastically taken up by the Spanish (whose social rules were stricter) and by some other European countries, notably France and England. It was a harmless diversion that must have passed away many a tedious evening, and it could be used at a distance with some eloquence.

5 Making and Repairing Fans

MAKING FANS

In appearance fans seem very fragile, like colourful butterflies which crush in the hand, and many new collectors wish to know how they are made.

In the late 1970s I was fortunate to be sent 19 colour transparencies showing a well-respected Japanese fan maker at work, together with a brief explanation of his techniques. Previous books have (nearly) all shown illustrations from Diderot's *Recueil de Planches sur les Sciences, les Arts Libéraux et les Arts Méchaniques* dated 1765 (to illustrate his encyclopaedia) but I feel it may be of interest to know how a modern Japanese fan master makes a folding fan today.

It seems that fan makers in eighteenth century Europe were generally women, whereas in the Orient they were generally men; in Europe they worked standing at trestle tables, while in Japan they were seated upon the floor. Mr Nakamura Kiyoe works on a shaped tree-trunk about 18 inches off the ground and about 18 inches across the roughly hewn surface, with all his materials spread around him in colourful disarray. His procedure for making a simple folding fan is as follows:

Two thin pieces of paper are glued together, after which they are painted with a design. The painting is often done with a blue dye, called *Gungyo*. Then the fan shape is cut out, and this basic shape of double paper is called *Washi*.

Two pieces of tanned, heavy-duty, pleated paper are then put to use; they are called *Kataji*, one side being called *Ogata*, the other *Megata*. The painted fan leaf (*washi*) is placed between the *kataji*, with the leaf being pleated between them, the fingers nipping the leaf home into each pleat. Then everything is separated and the fan leaf is re-pleated more firmly by itself, making knife edges.

As the *washi* is made from two thin pieces of paper glued together, it is necessary to part them in places for the sticks to be inserted within the pleats and evenly distanced. So a thin stick is inserted, up to a certain distance (in France this stick, or probe, was known as a *sonde* and was made of copper).

The next action is to cut along the edges of the folded paper leaf in order to neaten it, and to make a rice-paste glue (*Himenori*) for the bamboo sticks. These would have been supplied ready-made by other craftsmen, complete with a small metal rivet. When the glue is sufficiently kneaded it is rapidly brushed onto the upper part of the sticks, then the maker blows hard along the opened-up edge of the fan leaf and, with one swift, sure movement, the sticks are thrust into the fan leaf, one stick up each aperture. The fan is then left open to dry for a short while and is finally folded, ready for sale.

In Paris, during the nineteenth and early twentieth centuries, firms such as Lachelin and Duvelleroy used much the same process, except that the *kataji* were made from strong cardboard. In Japan all the interest was, and is, concentrated on the leaf of a fan; in Europe, including Spain, the interest was as much on the sticks and guards.

Spanish names for the parts of a fan are as follows: the leaf is *paise*, the sticks are *varetas*, the guards are *caberas*, the whole framework is *paquete*, the pin or rivet is *aboleta* and the area from the pin or head of the fan to the leaf is *fuente*. A good fan is an *abanico*, a cheap fan is a *chumbo* and brisé fans are called *baraja*.

Most people today associate fans with Spain (and bullfights) or Italy (and the opera). There is a small, thriving fanmaking industry in Italy and a far larger one in Spain where, apart from a few innovations in the form of modern machinery, the flourishing fan industry has altered little in the past 150 years.

It is reported that the mounting of the leaf in Spain was left in the hands of nimble-fingered women: one group would pleat the paper or textile into a cardboard mould; another group would cut with precision along the upper edge of the pleated leaf; another would glue the upper section of the sticks and rapidly insert them among the pleats of the leaf. Then the folded fan would be tied together with a fine cord and left to dry for a day—after which the edging was applied.

It was only then that the artist would decorate the fan. He might copy an established painting by a famous artist (using the old cartoon techniques of pricking the outline of a tracing with a pin and shaking fine black powder through the holes) or he might paint as he wished.

During the twentieth century it became established practice for the 'background flowers' to be painted in first, followed by the main decoration.

Most of the fans made in Spain during the earlier part of the nineteenth century had carved wooden sticks; pine, brought from the Province of Cuenca, being used for the most expensive fans, poplar for the cheaper ones. It is reported that the wood was soaked in water for several days to soften it, after which the shaped sticks were covered with a roughly painted paper leaf. Later on, lithographs and colour prints were mounted on both paper and silk, and as time went by, there were introduced into Spanish fans sticks and guards made from tortoiseshell, mother-of-pearl, horn, bone and ivory, all of which were worked by machine, with a fretsaw (*serreta*) which was foot-controlled, using a traced design and working on three sticks at a time. In the twentieth century the types of wood used in Spain widened to beach, banana, medlar, apple, pear, birch, ebony and sandalwood.

Working as a fan painter in the twentieth century was no sinecure and was very competitive. An original design might take up to a week to complete, being painted on kid or silk and bringing in up to 500 pesetas (in 1957). Bench-workers, on piecework, working all day with hardly a break, might earn themselves up to 150 pesetas a day, and the 'in-between' workers, who produced a medium-price quality, received a moderate but regular income. Top-quality work was very nerve-racking in spite of the prestige, while the cheapest work was boring in its repetitiveness, so the medium-price quality was the most favoured.

The making of extremely fine fans has been well-documented in previous books, but no one has written very much about fans made during the past 100 years. It must be obvious from the above that techniques have stabilised, especially as fans became cheaper, and it may be of interest to consider relative prices about a hundred years ago. In *c* 1880 it was quite possible to pay out as much as £100 for a fine 'dress fan' made in France or Germany. 'Common fans' made by the French in 1880 were priced at five pence a dozen; cockade fans were six pence each, telescopic fans could be bought for $2\frac{1}{2}$ pence. Japanese *uchiwa* were six pence each and Chinese painted gauze or silk fixed fans were one shilling and sixpence. But the cheapest fans of all were sold in Spain, where some might be bought for a farthing each.

XXVI. Spanish fan, the paper leaf showing a charming scene of the dance; the sticks are of bone overlaid with very small areas of gold leaf. 10¾″ : 27.5 cms. Mid-19th century. Private Collection.

XXVII. Spanish fan, with a very colourful scene of bull-fighting, etc., probably sold as a souvenir; wooden sticks. 13¾″ : 35 cms. Mid-19th century. Owned by Mrs Margaret Little.

XXVIII. Spanish fan, the paper leaf having a decoration on it of the entrance of the toreadors; wooden sticks. 13¾″ : 35 cms. c 1850. Owned by Mrs Margaret Little.

XXIX. Large folding fan: thin rust silk gauze mount, hand-painted with nasturtiums, buds and leaves; serpentine sticks and guards of wood. Signed 'Daillard'. 14″ : 35.75 cms. Probably French. c 1890–1900. Owned by Mrs Grace Grayson.

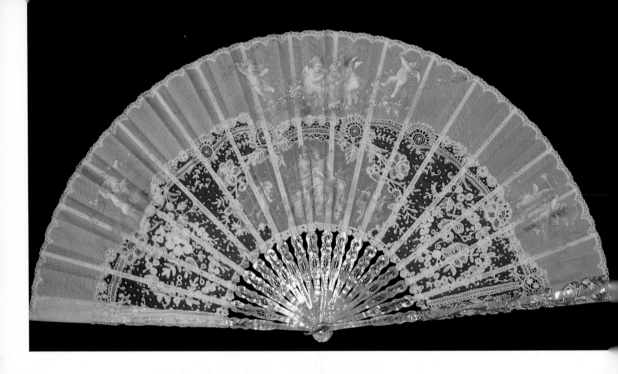

XXX. Mother-of-pearl fan with a leaf of silk gauze most delicately painted and inset with panels of Brussels needlepoint lace. 13¾″ : 35 cms. c 1860. Private Collection.

XXXI. Small sequinned and spangled fan which is very effective when carried at a dance. 8″ : 20.5 cms. Late 19th century. Owned by Mrs Margaret Little.

DISPLAYING FANS

The choice for fan collectors is either to display their fans or to put them away; this choice is entirely personal and there is no 'must' attached to either approach.

When displaying a fan the collector may mount it on a stand or may prefer to frame it. Putting it on a stand should only be a *very* temporary amusement—it would gather dust, dulling the materials, as well as being a magnet for interested fingers. If placed upon a stand (several shaped types are available), then a backing plate is absolutely essential for the fan to lean against—clear plastic is very suitable.

It is wisest to have a fan framed by a professional, for although it sounds easy enough to do, the project has many hidden pitfalls. Fans can be permanently damaged, drastically reducing their aesthetic and investment value, by a sloppy or unscrupulous framing job. The best way to protect your collection is to choose your framer with care; try hard to find a conscientious craftsman who can be trusted to use

43. The paper leaf is painted with a lover crowning his mistress: mounted on pierced, carved and painted ivory sticks. This would be magnificent displayed in a frame with a coloured background. Second half of the 18th century. Possibly German. $10\frac{1}{2}''$: 26.5 cms. By courtesy of Bonhams, Knightsbridge.

reliable materials.

Acidic materials are the greatest worry, but art must also be protected from light (especially sunlight), moisture, heat (never hang a framed fan over a fireplace or a radiator), air pollution, insects, handling and transport.

Be very careful about the cardboard borders used within a frame. Two kinds are generally available, a regular board and a rag board, and while the regular is sold in many enticing colours, it is very acidic and can do much harm to fan leaves of the past. Some form of cardboard, however, is essential, for it keeps the fan or fan leaf away from the glass which may contain injurious impurities; the board also creates a controlled air space without which you might get condensation, leading to water-spotting, mould and rot. There is also the danger that the illustration might actually stick to the glass.

Acid causes discolouration, brittleness and deterioration of paper and textiles, sometimes in a few months, sometimes in a few years, depending upon climatic conditions.

On the other hand rag board (or museum board, as it is also known) can be virtually free of acid. It is more expensive and the way to tell the difference is that, while rag board has a colouring which goes right the way through, regular board often has a sandwich of a different colour in the middle. Refuse the latter if you wish to care for your fan leaf.

The backing (the stiff board which holds the fan leaf) should, of course, be acid-free: it is always advisable to have a fan leaf mounted on rag board, treated wood or acid-free fabric. Also, when the whole fan or fan leaf is finally framed, make sure that no corrugated paper is used to seal the back; that, too, is filled with acid and would eventually show on the fan as brown stripes.

Light, especially sunlight, can be damaging to fan leaves or fans, so the type of glass used can be important. Good framers carry a wide choice, best of all being ultraviolet plexiglass which brings the work up to museum standards. It is very light in weight, looks like clear

44. *Top: an ivory brisé fan with central painted vignette of Venus and Cupid: the whole fan finely pierced and carved. This technique would be almost impossible to repair. French. c 1820. 10" : 25.5 cms. Bottom: a combination or repaired fan, the leaf painted in the 19th century, showing lovers in a landscape, the sticks of the 18th century, of carved, pierced and painted ivory. 11½" : 29 cms. By courtesy of Bonhams, Knightsbridge.*

45. *Chinese goose-feather fan tipped with maribou and painted with typical Canton School butterfly and flower scene, the sticks and guards are of well-carved ivory. It is accompanied by its box decorated with fine two-colour gold painting on a black lacquer background. Very great care has to be taken with these fans, for the paint can easily chip off – this is in a perfect condition. 11¼″ : 28.5 cms. Canton. c 1820.* From Fans of Imperial China *by* Neville Iröns, *by courtesy of the House of Fans Limited.*

glass and is expensive, but offers the greatest protection because it filters out harmful rays which cause fading and discolouration. Ordinary plexiglass, also light in weight, does not have the filtering power of UV but is good for very large areas. Both kinds of plexiglass have the disadvantage of attracting dust and being easy to scratch, so special cleaners are necessary. Non-glare glass (a recent fad) is also expensive but does not actually offer any extra protection and tends to obscure the image.

Mouldings are now available in an enormous variety of styles, widths, shapes and prices. It is always wise to go to a framer where the work is done on the premises and where the primary interest is in the preservation of fans and fan leaves. Most good framers believe that the frame should enhance the fan and be chosen 'from the fan out', rather than 'from the room (where it is to be hung) out'.

It is wisest to go to some specialist fan framer rather than to a local firm dealing mainly with prints and photographs. The specialist knows which backing materials would harmonise and be correct for the age of the fan, and can also deal with such problems as the width of the rivet and the weight of the guards, so that the fan or fan leaf may be withdrawn from the frame at a later date, for exhibition or for sale, in the same condition as when you acquired it. Your framer will also advise on whether it would be better to have a rectangular-shaped frame or a fan-shaped frame, in order to blend in with all the other framed works of art in your home.

When discussing with a framer or repairer the work to be done, it is better to supply too many details than too few. Give the measurements, a description, the colouring (an instant photograph is most useful) and, when writing, enclose a self-addressed stamped envelope; do not be afraid to enquire about prices for, as you can see from the above, they would vary a good deal, depending upon the quality of the materials required.

There are several people in Britain who frame fans and it would be sensible to pick the one nearest to yourself; it is never wise to send anything through the regular post, far better to travel with your precious fan and speak to your framer yourself. In that way there can be no confusion over backing fabrics, colours, frame mouldings and prices; for both your sakes it is also a good idea to have all these details enumerated on paper.

For both repairing and framing I can recommend, from personal experience:

Peter J. Greenhalgh
87 Church Road
Shoeburyness
Essex

I would write to him in the first instance and then, should it be convenient to you both, arrangements might be made to meet. Don't hurry the repair or framing of a fan: it has, after all, been in existence for many, many years and it would be a false economy to expect a deadline now. Once your fan is repaired or framed it is obviously going to enhance its value and give it many more years of life, so it is worth being patient. In this way you will find a charming relationship building up between yourself and the specialist craftsman, for a repairer of fans, with the multitude of materials involved, is often a repairer of most small antiques and therefore extremely useful to know.

STORING FANS

When you store a fan it is as well to remember the danger points raised above: light, moisture, heat, insects and handling. Firstly you should carefully fold the fan, seeing that none of the ribbons have doubled back upon themselves, and then wrap it gently but firmly in a double sheet of acid-free white tissue paper. Use a large sheet, so that both ends of the fan are covered and the paper is folded back over the fan. It is not wise to use a rubber band which, over the months, would put a strain on some part—the tissue paper should hold it if you use enough. Don't worry about the inevitable creases, but be careful to keep the paper clean because dirt usually comes from fingermarks and there is little grime more acid than the perspiration on the fingers.

The container in which you plan to store your fans must then be prepared. Should you be fortunate enough to have a specialist fan cabinet you will find there is depth for only one fan to be placed flat in each compartment, rather than fans lying on top of each other in an ordinary drawer. But first you must ensure that the drawer, wherever it is, is free of insects or fungus. Treat the drawer with a fungicide/bactericide in any case, for some bacteria or mites are hardly visible and you would be amazed if you knew how much animal life you are entertaining in your home, however clean. I suggest either *SOPP* or *Mystox LPL*, both available from *Picreator Enterprises Ltd, 44 Park View Gardens, London NW4 2PN*; or *Talas, 213 West 35th Street, New York, NY 10001–1 966*; or *Conservation Materials Ltd., 240 Freeport Boulevard, PO Box 2884, Sparks, Nevada 89431, USA.*

Some museum experts suggest that you then line your drawer with velvet, holding it down with an adhesive, so that the tissue-paper-wrapped fans do not slide up and down the drawer each time it is opened or shut. Lastly, you should guard against damp in the drawer. In order to find out if any damp is there, you can make up some small gauze or net bags of *Silica Gel* and place them permanently in a corner of the drawer. *Silica Gel* (ask for the special self-indicating type at a chemist or photographers) is a crystalline substance which absorbs atmospheric moisture in a closed container, changing colour from blue to pink as it reaches its saturation point. Once it has turned pink you can re-use it by warming it in a very cool oven, which drives off the moisture and restores the original blue tint. You can also buy *Silica Gel* from the specialist firm mentioned above which makes conservation materials for most of the museums of the world.

REPAIRING FANS
Many collectors have to decide whether they wish to repair a damaged fan, whether it should be conserved (conservation is virtually the museum technique of a reversible repair and, obviously, although extremely costly, the best choice) or whether merely to clean it.

I have given a complete chapter on 'The Repair of Fans' in *The Book of Fans* which has, I understand, helped many amateurs to set up a small workshop. However, if a new collector wishes to tidy up a recent purchase on a strictly limited scale, the following may be of assistance.

Fans need to be cleaned when bought, and care taken over both leaf and sticks. Each material should be considered separately, and a decision made as to whether to leave it alone or not. Unhappily, many owners in the past used stamp hinges to hold a fan leaf together, or, since the last war, an impact adhesive; this must first be completely removed (*Dissolvex* is good) with infinite patience, and then the damage assessed.

Most dirt is a strange mixture of dust, fluff, food and perspiration

XXXII. *Japanese Export fan, rigid and asymetrical, made from bamboo covered with soft paper, embossed with 'ribs'. The flowers are cunningly made from silk with no stitching at all. The handle is solid and there is a signature of the artist. Approx. 12″ × 11″ (30.5 cms × 28 cms). c 1890–1903. Owned by Mrs Grace Grayson.*

XXXIII. *Two Japanese ogi (folding fans). This illustration shows the obverse of one fan (on the left) and the reverse of another. They are delicate paintings in watercolours and gold leaf on a leaf made from a silk and paper mixture. The sticks are of plain, polished, 'tea-stick' bamboo, serrated along the edges; the guards are of ivory with shibayama inlay and cut off sharply and squarely – both the serrations and the 'squared-off' look are typically Japanese. 10¾″ : 27.5 cms. c 1875. From* Fans of Imperial Japan *by Neville Irons, by courtesy of The House of Fans Limited.*

XXXIV. *Zōge ogi, decorated in varying shades of gold (takamaki-e and hiramaki-e), the guards having shibayama inlay; there is a long cord with a double tassel. These fans were only made between 1860–1885. Japanese, for the Export market. 9½" : 24 cms. Owned by Mrs Geraldine Pember.*

XXXV. *Empire fan leaf. The subject, painted upon silk, is that of Orpheus (seated) with his lyre, accompanied by Eurydice, seen in a Neo-classical interior with columns of foil, statues, vases, etc., embellished with different sizes of gilt sequins and gilt embroidery. c 1800. Author's Collection.*

XXXVI. Marriage fans in action! The bride is Wendy Alves, seen recently with her attendants in California, all carrying flowers and ribbons with their fans. The flowers, fans and design were by Mrs Geraldine Pember, the photograph by Juliette Ohleyer in Orinda, California.

XXXVII. Spangled fan, embroidered with silver spangles and sequins on net, with mother-of-pearl sticks and guards decorated with cut-steels 'piqué-point'. English or French. 19th century. $9\frac{1}{2}''$: 24.25 cms. Owned by Mrs Margaret Little.

XXXVIII. Spanish fan, the paper leaf decorated with bull-fighting scenes. The sticks of pierced aromatic wood and cut-steels 'piqué-point'. $10\frac{1}{2}''$: 26.75 cms. 19th century. Owned by Mrs Margaret Little.

XXXIX. Articulated fan, the leaf printed with a 'Watteau-esque' design, the sticks and guards of bone. A tiny pin, half-way down the guard, pushes upwards and a small mirror emerges from the top of the guard – not so much to check on the lady's appearance, but more to discover if a gentleman is hovering behind her. $8\frac{1}{2}''$: 21.5 cms. Late 19th century. Private Collection.

XL. Edwardian fan, the leaf being backed with netting, embellished with gilt spangles and sequins; the sticks and guards are of mother-of-pearl. $8\frac{1}{2}''$: 21.5 cms. Private Collection.

all bonded together over the years; in many cases it is actually holding the fan together, in some it can come off in a solid piece, in others it has to be removed by stages. When it has all gone the underlying material may be found to be too fragile without new support.

I would suggest to the new collector that, on the whole, the fan leaf should be left alone, apart from carefully brushing off surface dust with a clean, soft brush. The specialist repairer can work miracles (and there are many techniques) but the new owner is wise to leave well alone.

Fan sticks could, in some cases, be cleaned by the amateur, using a magnifying glass and a strong light. If the sticks are made from ivory there are two basic methods to follow: either knead a substance such as *Groom/stick* into all the crevices (available at *Picreator*, above) or clean with a minute amount of distilled water on a cotton-wool-covered orange-stick. *Groom/stick* looks a little like putty when warmed in the hand and, if sufficiently supple from the warmth, it can be gently pushed into every crevice of the carving and then peeled off, taking the dirt with it. It can be used again and again. Otherwise the ivory sticks may be cleaned, one section at a time, with distilled water (never water from the tap). Both these techniques apply as well to tortoise-shell, bone, horn and mother-of-pearl.

Having cleaned the sticks and allowed them to rest and dry out completely (moisture is the greatest danger) it is wise to preserve them with a little *Mystox* solution as a fungicide/bactericide/insecticide, followed by *Renaissance* wax polish to give the sticks a faint sheen and protection for about ten years. (Both solutions are available from *Picreators* and the wax polish is on sale in many good stores, too.)

If any of the sticks happen to be broken, a new collector should ask the advice of a professional before embarking on any repairs. Only after years of actually handling fans do owners feel competent to try to repair their own fans, not just because of the techniques but also because of the stress points on the fan; an inexperienced collector could break a stick while working on the leaf, purely through ignorance of the crucial balance and stress areas on a certain type of fan.

On the whole it is acceptable to collectors to remove grime but not to add anything, such as touching up a painted decoration, because today's paints are rather different from those originally employed. The scene might look much better to begin with but, after a short time, it would be obvious where the new paints had been used.

The same applies to the use of new textiles, lace and so on: if a textile is to be repaired, then a textile of the same period should be used from another fan which is past repair.

It cannot be stressed too much that a new collector should try to avoid buying a fan which needs repairing; if she has done so (and paid a lot for it) she should seek out a specialist repairer instead of embarking on the work herself. There are quite a few in most countries and the Fan Societies generally have some names on their books and can advise. If, on the other hand, the new owner is absolutely determined to carry out repairs herself, there are two basic rules: make an appointment with the conservation department of the best local museum to get specialist advice and then, if in any doubt at all about her capabilities—DON'T.

THE BACKGROUND TO AN INDUSTRY

It is curious that the countries which made fans in the past, and to which we give the loudest praise, are those which have no fan industries today; the one country that fan collectors have rather denigrated, and whose fans fetch the lowest prices, now has the major production . . . Spain. Fans from France, England, Italy, Holland and the Low Countries, Germany, Austria, Russia and Switzerland have been written up in much detail in former books—as well as fans from the Orient. However, very little has been written about factory production in Spain until now and, as Spanish fans are available for the new collector, and are reasonably priced, it may be of interest to study them here.

In Manuel Rocamora's book on fans the frontispiece illustrates a magnificent banner (or flag) fan, embroidered with gold thread and sequins, showing the coat of arms of Barcelona. This was originally owned by the Marqués dell Valle de Ribas (General Llander) who was Capitán General of Cataluña, and was made in the first quarter of the fourteenth century. In museums throughout Spain there are collections of fans to be studied—in Madrid there are fine ones at the Prado, the Museo Lazaro Galdiano (Calle Maria de Molina) and the Museo de Historia Traje (Museum of History of Costume) at Aranjuez. Some other famous and noteworthy collections are the Pirozzini, the Sedó-Ragull, the Somzeé and the Piogey.

During 1920 the Spanish Society of the Friends of Art mounted an exhibition in Madrid, followed by a further one in Barcelona in 1922. In 1946, in Madrid, in the Exhibition of Decorative Arts (organised by the Union of Arts and Crafts) there was a stand of fans (many from the Sedó-Ragull Collection) as well as a demonstration by a group of craftsmen from a fan workshop in Valencia. In 1953 there was another stand of fans at the International Exhibition of Arts and Crafts in Madrid. These were sent in by the best manufacturers of Valencia, amongst them the workshops of Barber y Lorca, Colomina, Albinana, Claphes and the fan factory of Jose Prior—famed (and honoured) for his work in the manufacture of tortoiseshell objects, especially those artistic Spanish combs.

Naturally fans had always been used in the Summer heat of Spain and there are innumerable records of early ones. In the Inventory of Bartolome Arbella, Valencia, 18th August 1429, for instance, is the following: 'Idem dos ventalls de palma guarnits de aluda' (Item: two palmetto fans decorated with lambskin).

In the light of Spain's complicated history, it is really no surprise that a fan industry was not established there until the nineteenth century. The first factories started under French influence (M. Coustellier from Paris was virtually the first to establish a factory in c 1830); many more opened during a long period of female rule (Isabella 1833–1868, the Regent from 1833–1841 being her mother, Maria Cristina) and during the general period of stability from 1875–1923. It was not until the early 1880s that a Spanish economist felt happy to write, 'Without being a rich country Spain has become comfortably off.'

One should consider, very briefly, the history of the Philippines as well, for much cheap labour and materials were imported from there when it was a Spanish Colony. Manila, the capital city, is 700 miles South East of Hong Kong and was a walled Muslim settlement during the sixteenth century—much Muslim-inspired decoration is seen on Spanish fans. Manila was invaded by the Chinese in 1574, raided by the Dutch in the mid-seventeenth century, colonised by the Spaniards in 1751, held briefly by the British in 1762, restored to Spain in 1763, opened to foreign trade in 1832 and then taken over by the Americans after the Spanish-American War of 1898. As a result there was an Irish-stew of influences.

Some highly individual fans were made in Spain during the eighteenth century, but they were all 'one-off'. One very popular one was the mask or domino type, with a central painted face, the eyes cut out to look through and the remainder of the fan decorated with drawings of goats, butterflies and flowers. Another type was the topographical fan, and there are fans extant showing views of the City of Madrid and the City of Barcelona. Another I have seen is a printed fan, hand coloured, showing a concert in the theatre in Madrid ('Concierto de Musica de las Serenatas executadas en Madrid en la Caresma pasada').

It is well known that, before this time, the Spaniards imported their fans in bulk from France, England and the Netherlands. I am indebted to Betty Hodgkinson for the information that the *Companion Guide to the Museum of History of Costume* at Aranjuez, outside Madrid, states that, in 1792, imports of fans from France alone numbered 652,720. I was interested, too, to come across a fan published by C. Sloper of London (early nineteenth century) showing the coats of arms of England and Spain, with a central medallion showing Fernando VII.

A Royal Fan Factory is known to have existed in Valencia in 1802, in the Plaza de Cajeros; during that year, for the visit of Carlos IV and Maria Luisa, the firm made some outstanding illuminated addresses in their honour, as well as some interesting fans. It is also recorded that one of the first industrialists to found a factory in Valencia was Don Jose Colomina, from Jijona in Alicante, around 1840. He imported his silks from France, which were woven by the Valencian 'vellutera', and he made sufficient really artistic fans 'to satisfy the market.' He was eventually elevated to Marqués de Colomina. At around the same time a French craftsman, Simonet (representing the Parisian firm of Colombert), set up in Valencia what were probably some of the best workshops of the period, called Bernad & Riace; it is known that he employed the free-lance craftsmen Puchol and Chafarandas, amongst others.

At a slightly later date the great master, Jose Prior, started a factory in Valencia, which in time rivalled that of Colomina. Don Jose Maria Prior Sanchis (to give his full name) became the President of the Industria Abaniquera in Valencia, and by 1900, when he was about 40 years old, his workshop and factory in Paseo de la Pechina were very famous. His sons, Jose and Salvador, were his best assistants. Then, in 1905, the King of Spain visited Valencia, paid the factory a visit and appointed Jose Prior Purveyor to the Royal Household, honouring him with the Cruz de Caballero de la Orden de Isabel la Catolica.

Yet another factory in Valencia (where most fans were made) was that of Don Joaquin Forteza who had his mounting and painting workshops in Calle Quemadero at the beginning of the twentieth century. His fans were very fine, and amongst his artists and craftsmen were his two sons (Joaquinto and Paco), Enrique Perez (an excellent copyist of the great artists of the 16th century), Vincente Esteve, celebrated for his paintings on kidskin, Pacorret, who specialised in flowers, Fransiquet, who lived in Godella, the village of the artists, and Professor Almela Mengot. A contemporary manufactory was that of the Mañas Brothers: they had their premises in Alameditas de Serranos, with a great many craftsmen working for them and a reputation of being among the most wealthy.

Until the Civil War there were also the workshops of Antonio Blanquer, Ricardo Badenes, Juan Quer Claphes, Barber y Lorca, Vicente Albinana, Castillo, Llorens, Estelles, Roig y Bergada and Caballer y Navarro.

There are copious records of the various craftsmen involved in the industry. Outstanding makers of sticks and guards were: Reig, Gimeno, Mateu, Puchol Nina, Balaguer, Sancho, Garefa and Peris; famous decorators and painters were: Ruano Llopis, Canet, Barrena, Vercher, Ballester, Guillot, Biago, Badia, Enrique Perez, Martinez Bianquer, Alonso and Sanchis. Spanish fan production, as a whole, reached a peak from 1833–1898, dipped down in the 1920s and rose again after the Spanish Civil War. Today there are many fan shops and fan factories in Spain, too numerous to enumerate, and they export all over the world, from the Philippines to most of the South American countries.

Of great interest are the subjects, many of them printed, chosen by the Spanish makers to decorate their fans; a proud race, they commemorated many events in their country. One fan showed Alphonso XII comforting victims of the Andalusian earthquake of 1884; another portrayed the same King in a central illustration, together with the crown, with the words in two vignettes, 'Nacio el 28 de noviembre de 1857 en Madrid' and 'Proclamado el 29 de diciembre de 1874 en Sagunto (Valencia).' One splendid example marked the country's first railway train, near Valencia; another showed King Amadeo I embarking on a ship at Cartagena, while yet another celebrated 'the improvements of the century'.

Many Spanish fans show the steps of dances, such as the mazurka; several illustrate scenes from Rossini's operas, and there are endless examples extant commemorating the Constitution of 1812. Very few that have been seen in exhibitions show the 'souvenir' type of bullfighting scene; most of the better quality fans were either political or nationalistic.

The Spaniards made fans from lace, too. During the eighteenth century good quality lace was generally imported from France (Chantilly was the most popular for mantillas and fans), and before that from the Spanish-dominated Netherlands. At the beginning of the nineteenth century, however, blonde and black blonde silk lace (lace undyed and unbleached, and lace dyed black) was made in Catalonia and La Mancha, the silk being spun near Barcelona. Various lace-making centres at different times have produced laces in the Spanish style, generally a somewhat heavier type than usual. Later, machine-made lace was produced for fans, and that is what is bought today.

There is very little written about fans in Spain (currently only one book is on sale there—a translation of one of my own), so reference must be made to entries in encyclopaedias or introductions to exhibition catalogues. This is very curious for a country with a thriving industry—albeit a fairly modern one. There is also a notable political bias: the various authors never refer to French or English published material, but only to the 1884 Exhibition in Milan or the 1891 Exhibition in Karlsruhe. All collectors would welcome a thoroughly researched book on Spanish fans, especially one that compared them to other European fans of the same period.

Spanish fans can be interesting and unusual (I was delighted to be sent details of various advertising fans by Gillian Troche, who deals in fans at Washington, Sussex) but the run-of-the-mill fans are pretty deadly. Most nineteenth and twentieth-century examples are prints, lithographs or stipple engravings, easily recognisable and with rather garish colours. What often identifies them is the curious proportion of the leaf to the sticks—they are rarely what one would expect, i.e. they may be three-fifths of the total length, instead of a quarter or half, giving one a sense of mathematical syncopation. Spanish fans can be identified by their sticks and guards as well: the materials were more often than not a cheap version of something good—bone in place of ivory, horn in place of tortoiseshell, and woods encrusted with shiny

46. *This nineteenth century fan with a printed leaf shows four albumen print portrait photographs and three view photographs, believed to be related to a Paraguayan Revolution, mounted on pierced bone sticks. Probably made in Spain. c 1850/60. 10" : 25.5 cms. By courtesy of Bonhams, Knightsbridge.*

cut steels. Better Spanish fans exhibit a lot of thick, gilt, white mother-of-pearl which becomes extemely heavy in the hand.

All the same, for the new collector, it is still very possible to buy colourful Spanish fans of the nineteenth century, and it may well be that Spanish fans of the eighteenth century, discovered in some little-known place, will become the prized centrepiece of some future collection.

47. Nineteenth-century 'Cabriolet' fan of hand-
painted silk, the lower leaf signed Y. Serand. *Sticks
and guards of tortoiseshell. Possibly French.*
9½″ : 24 cms. *The owner dates this c 1830. Owned by
Mrs Geraldine Pember. As this has neither a
cabriolet painted upon this unusual fan, nor any
other form of transport, it should technically be
termed a 'double-leafed' fan as it is of the 19th
century.*

6 Guilds

European cities, in medieval days, were the natural habitat of the bourgeoisie, merchants and specialised craftsmen; an oligarchy of competence, they became forced to organise their agglomerations. Out of ignorance and chaos they created a system of municipal administration for free men living together—and thus, in time, helped to end the ancient feudal systems.

They elected their own town officials headed by their greatest man, their 'mair'—from the Latin 'major' or 'maior', meaning 'greater'—a word which eventually became 'mayor'. To assist him they elected the elder statesmen of the city, the 'elders' or, later, 'aldermen'; and they all met to discuss business sitting round a slab of wood which nowadays we call a table but which, in those days, was merely called 'the board' ... resulting in the phrase 'The Mayor and Board of Aldermen'.

Eventually the educated bourgeoisie infiltrated the office-holding class, providing many notaries, lawyers and accountants; they acquired such a standing that they were often entertained by kings. The bourgeoisie had a very strong civic sense and this could expand, in time, to become a national patriotism. Some countries (such as modern Germany or Italy) have come late to this; they did not acquire a national identity until fairly recently and, at times of stress, some of their national leaders still think with a regional spirit. But amongst themselves it was generally agreed that, on the basis of a very strong moral background, 'if you worked hard and long hours and wisely weighed up your decisions, then you would become wealthy and honoured by your fellow citizens; the poor were merely contemptuous layabouts.'

The backbone of medieval economy was the guild (the word first appears in Charlemagne's decrees) which had strong religious overtones. In England the guilds, religious associations of men with similar mercantile interests, were established to provide mutual aid, protection, a moral standard and better times. The same applied in France until they rejected their faith.

At first there was one guild to a town, but as the population grew and interests were diverted into differing channels, the guilds divided: vertically into the merchant-owners and the workers, employers and employees, rich and poor; horizontally into crafts or trade guilds and sometimes separated by distinctions as narrow as some of the union branches of Britain today. The obvious purpose was to promote the economic welfare of each member of each guild and to guarantee him full employment at high wages by restricting membership. The guild regulated work procedures and hours of labour, it set maximum wages (not minimum) and standardised quality, it promoted discipline and solidarity and set out to preserve the status quo. But it also restricted its members in many ways: it forbade price-cutting, overtime work, public advertising and the introduction of new tools . . . its aim, therefore, was in fact control. (One of the most brilliant word pictures of mercantile life in late-medieval times is *The Merchant of Prato* by Iris Origo.)

Guilds extracted dues from their members and some became very rich, owning property, having their own chapels in great churches and cathedrals, looking after the stricken living (widows, children or invalids) and contributing to the arts through gifts to churches or by producing the 'Mystery Plays' (from the Latin 'mysterium', meaning 'full of or wrapt in mystery').

These plays were about the miracles of Christ and in medieval times were traditionally acted out only by members of guilds. 'The Art or Mistery of Fanmaking' comes from another Latin word 'ministerium', which is quite different and means 'service, occupation or handicraft'.

In France the making of fans became of such importance during the reign of Henry the Great (who came to the throne in 1598 and was assassinated in 1610) that in 1594 several bodies of craftsmen were granted certain concessions, others being added in 1664. In 1673 the master fan makers of the City of Paris presented a petition to King Louis XIV and they were constituted a corporate body in that year. Sixty masters became the nucleus, fighting for their privileges, which became further strengthened by new edicts in 1676 and 1678, decreeing that no one could become a master without first serving a four-year apprenticeship and then producing his 'master's piece' which must pass the test of craftsmanship. The company was ruled by four jurors, two of whom were re-nominated each year by an assembly in which every master could participate. The entrance fee to the company was 400 livres and widows were permitted to continue their late husband's businesses as long as they remained single, as well as being granted various other privileges. By the middle of the eighteenth century, when fanmaking reached a peak in France, 150 Master Fan Makers were recorded in the City of Paris alone, protected and assisted by their guild regulations.

On 27th August, 1789, the Constituent Assembly of France adopted the Declaration of the Rights of Man and of the Citizen. The great desideratum of the bourgeoisie was 'freedom' in its public and political aspects; with 'freedom', the Declaration closely associated 'equality', demanded by the bourgeoisie in opposition to the aristocracy and by the peasants in the face of the feudal lords. The Declaration held that the law was to be the same for everyone and all citizens were equal in its eyes. The entire country went through a political and administrative upheaval and, in March 1791, the Allarde Law abolished journeymen's associations, guilds, secret societies and privileged manufacturers as well. The national market was unified by the abolition of customs dues and tolls. Finally there was freedom of work, with every individual free to create and produce, to pursue profit and to employ it as he desired. To a certain extent the fanmaking industry was shattered in France and it took some years to re-stabilise; sadly, for historians, so many records carefully kept by the many guilds were then lost or deliberately destroyed in the face of this new freedom.

Unhappily there were no fan guilds in the German States, which deprives us of much essential information.

The guilds of the City of London (that is, the part of London which is within the ancient boundaries, not the whole area which is called 'London' today), under the jurisdiction of the Lord Mayor and Corporation, had existed for many years before Edward III came to the throne in 1327; during his reign he made their powers and privileges much more definite and he himself became a member of the Merchant Taylors Company.

It was at that time that some of the guilds chose to call themselves 'companies' to differentiate themselves from other guilds, after which they began to wear a distinctive dress or 'livery'; as a result, they came to be called 'Livery Companies'. To this day the Mercers appear in dark red edged with fur, the Haberdashers in dark blue edged with fur and the Drapers in blue and yellow.

Nowadays there are about 84 Livery Companies in the City of London, although in some cases members have drifted away from being directly concerned with a certain type of trade; many men are Liverymen of various Companies either through business or family connections, treating them like social clubs with a strong charitable bias.

The 'Great Twelve' are the Mercers, Grocers, Drapers, Fishmongers, Goldsmiths, Skinners, Merchant Taylors, Haberdashers, Salters, Ironmongers, Vintners and Clothworkers . . . food and clothing taking pre-eminence.

In the past these Livery Companies generally had their own Halls in which they met or gave banquets; before the last World War there were 36 important examples, showing extremely interesting architecture over the decades, but 19 Halls were destroyed and a further 15 badly damaged by enemy bombing.

For the greater part of its history the British Worshipful Company of Fan-Makers had no fixed habitation but held its meetings in sundry taverns in the City of London. Until the outbreak of the Second World War it received hospitality from one or other of the old Livery Companies possessing their own halls.

The Worshipful Company of Fan-Makers were granted their Charter during the reign of Her Majesty Queen Anne. It is dated 19th April, 1709, and was enrolled in the Chamber of Guildhall of the City of London on 5th October, 1710, by the then Lord Mayor, Sir Samuel Garrard, Baronet, and the Court of Aldermen. The Fan-Makers Company is thus the youngest of the 'old' City Guilds, engaging in its craft of 'The Art or Mistery of Fanmaking'.

In 1941 the Court met for the first time in the Upper Room of the reconstructed St Dionis Hall, Lime Street, and dined in the hall itself. In 1952 the Company was accorded certain rights for the use of the parish hall of St Botolph's Church, Bishopsgate. As a result the Company extensively restored the hall; it was rededicated by the Bishop of Willesden and re-opened on 23rd October, 1952, by Her Royal Highness the Princess Alice, Duchess of Gloucester. This parish church hall is now known also as the Hall of the Worshipful Company of Fan-Makers.

The furnishing of the hall is in keeping with the history of the Company. The oak panelling dates back to 1726, the curtains being of a very old Tudor design against the rich contrasting colours of the silk banners of Arms belonging to certain Past Masters of the Company (many of whom had served the high office of Lord Mayor of London).

The emblem of their ancient craft of the fan is encased in a frame made from the timbers of the Guildhall destroyed by enemy action in 1940 and set in the panelling above the marble fireplace, surmounted by a carved Royal Coat of Arms.

The fan so portrayed is a fine copy of the Ostrich Fan presented to Her Majesty Queen Elizabeth, The Queen Mother, at the time of her Coronation. Below this, on a small autograph fan, are the signatures and autographs (dating from the time of Queen Victoria) of those members of the Royal Family to whom the Company has presented a fan to commemorate some historic or special occasion. This fan has now had every blade signed, so a new autograph fan was commissioned by the Fan-Makers in order to start afresh. It has been made by a firm in Madrid from a set of undecorated, overlapping nineteenth century ivory sticks with a simple, blank skin leaf of approximately the same age. The Arms of the Worshipful Company of Fan-Makers have been carved on a separate piece of ivory, lightly engraved, and then applied near the top of the guardstick. Members of the Royal Family who sign it do so with an antique quill-pen owned by the Company: the first signature on this new autograph fan is yet to be written—perhaps on the occasion of the next Coronation?

At the south end of the hall, over the entrance, is a stained-glass window depicting the arms of the Company. On either side of the entrance, on the panelling, are inscribed the names of the Masters since the Company's inception. For reasons of security the original Charter of the Company cannot be displayed, but a photocopy, suitably framed, is on view on the oak screen in front of the entrance and behind the chair in which the Master sits during Court meetings. Above the Charter is the coat of arms of Queen Anne, the Company's Charter Queen.

Although about 275 years does not sound a long time, the Company has distinguished itself with many Royal occasions. In 1897 HM Queen Victoria was presented with a fan to mark the occasion of her Diamond Jubilee; coronations were similarly marked in 1902 for Queen Alexandra, in 1911 for Queen Mary, in 1937 for Queen Elizabeth and in 1953 for our present Queen Elizabeth. Weddings, too, were prettily expressed with fans for HRH the Princess Mary in 1922, HRH the Princess Elizabeth in 1947, HRH the Princess Margaret in 1960, HRH the Princess Alexandra in 1963, HRH the Princess Richard of Glouces-ter in 1972, HRH the Princess Anne in 1973, and finally Diana, Princess of Wales in 1981.

Royalty must, by tradition, ask permission to enter into the City of London which is very jealous of its ancient rights and prerogatives. The greatest person in the City of London is the Lord Mayor and no less than six Masters of the Worshipful Company of Fan-Makers have been Lords Mayor since 1888. These are: Sir James Whitehead, Bart (Master 1884, Sheriff 1884 and Lord Mayor in 1888), Sir Alfred James Newton, Bart (Sheriff 1888, and having the twin honour of being both Master and Lord Mayor in 1899), Sir John Pound, Bart (Master in 1891, Sheriff 1895 and Lord Mayor in 1904), Sir John Bell, Bart (Master 1897, Sheriff 1901 and Lord Mayor in 1907), Sir Stephen Killick (Mas-ter 1917, Sheriff 1922 and Lord Mayor in 1934) and finally Colonel Sir Charles Davis, Bart (Sheriff 1942, Lord Mayor 1945 and Master in 1946).

The Company have not only played their part socially but have also acted within the framework of City Livery Companies. They have their main role, however, as the authorititive body of the Fan-Makers. Their list of bye-laws (which are still in use) was formed in 1741; most unfortunately their earliest Minutes only date from 1775, but it must have been an enthralling moment when, in 1951, one of the Company's chests was found complete with the original Charter of 1709, the bye-laws of 1710 and 1741 and an old Bible of 1726.

The Company's motto is 'Arts and Trade United' and this has genui-nely been their aim throughout their history, especially their object of protecting the English Fan-Maker in the eighteenth century when so many of the French Fan-Makers came over to London, either for religious reasons (the Huguenots were nearly always the finest crafts-men in France and the 1689 Revocation of the Edict of Nantes drove out many of them) or merely to satisfy the burgeoning English market for fine fans. The Company's historic Minutes make fascinating read-ing but they still keep their traditions with the trade by providing three bursaries or prizes.

48. Original Pump Room, Interior, Bath. 1737. Copper-engraving 187 × 428 mm, attributed to George Speren. Both Speren and Pinchbeck produced fan views of Bath, the former at

the Fan and Crown in the Grove, Bath: the latter at the Fan and Crown in the New Round Court in the Strand, London. By courtesy of the Victoria Art Gallery, Bath City Council.

To encourage the arts there is the Latchford Prize, Bronze Medal and Money Award: this is open to students of the Royal Academy School of Art, City of London Schools and other recognised bodies, and given once every three years for 'A Design for a Painted Fan or Monochrome'. A Member of the Fan Circle International, Peter Greenhalgh, won this Prize in 1981 and subsequently mounted the painted design on to suitable sticks for the Fan-Makers.

To encourage the rather more prosaic and technical 'machine to agitate the air' there is a Silver Medal and money prize now awarded to the best student of the year of the Fan Engineering section of the National College of Heating, Ventilating, Refrigeration and Fan Engineering.

Finally there is a Bursary or Scholarship awarded in connection with wind-tunnel or other aeronautical research work at the Cranfield Institute of Technology . . . which is about as up to date as one could go.

Many of the names mentioned above are disembodied people, distanced from us by time and by stature, so how can we relate to them and clothe them with flesh and blood? I have been fortunate in my friendship with Mr and Mrs Anthony Vaughan to whom I am enormously grateful for permission to reproduce some material which Anthony Vaughan had researched for a book, which may help bring to life an ordinary citizen of London.

Anthony Vaughan is, in many ways, a great link with the past. He is a Fan-Maker (although a Solicitor by occupation) and also a Member of the Fan Circle International, and he is within a long and continuing line of Vaughans who have been Fan-Makers since its Charter. Tony wrote a most fascinating book on the Georgian actress, Hannah Pritchard, also an ancestor of his, and her Fan-Maker brother (Edward Vaughan) who was well-known in his time; his account places in context the role of the fan and the actress during the eighteenth century when European fanmaking was at its peak. (*Born to Please: Hannah Pritchard, Actress, 1711–1768—A Critical Biography* by Anthony Vaughan, 1979). He wrote:

Of Hannah's three brothers Edward, the eldest, was born in or about 1704/5. In 1717 his father apprenticed him to a Japanner, Edward Wootton of St Martin's in the Fields, at a premium of £15, and on 21st December, 1725, he was admitted to the Fan-Makers Company (Admission Number 682).

He first set up business in Playhouse Yard, Drury Lane, in premises adjoining the Theatre, but eight years later (in 1733) he moved to Russell Court, Drury Lane. It was from the Golden Fan near the Chapel in Russell Court that Edward advertised his Necromantic Fan in the *Craftsman* for Saturday, 3rd August, 1734:

By Eo, Meo, & Areo,
On Monday last was published.
The Necromantic Fan, or Magick Glass.
Being a new-invented Machine Fan, that by a
slight Touch unseen a Lady in the Fan changes her
Dressing-Glass according to the following invitations:

If anyone himself would see,
Pray send the gentleman to me;
For in my Magick Glass I show
The Pedant, Poet, Cit or Beau;
Likewise a Statesman wisely dull,
Whose plodding Head's with Treaties full.
Etc.

Made and sold by Edward Vaughan,
Fanmaker, at the Golden Fan near the Chapel in Russell Court,
Drury Lane.

In July 1736 he obtained the Freedom of the City by redemption and moved again to premises adjoining the Royal Exchange, Cornhill, being the second house east from Sweetings Alley. A contemporary print of the Royal Exchange dated 1741 (after a drawing by Maurer) shows Edward Vaughan's shop in great detail in the foreground. It is represented as a tall, narrow five-storey building, the ground floor occupied by a double-fronted shop with bow windows. The fans can be seen clearly displayed for sale behind the small panes and over the entrance is a large carved wooden or plaster fan in a decorative cartouche. Two ladies have just left the shop and are proudly displaying the fans they have purchased.

Watches can also be seen hanging in the window of Mr Creake the clockmaker next door. Edward Vaughan or one of his assistants is leaning from a first floor window. There is another view taken some fifteen years later and published by Bowles which shows in addition an elaborate sign painted with a fan.

An insurance policy issued by the Hand in Hand in 1746 further complements and confirms this description. The house measured twelve feet six inches (frontage) by thirty-four feet (depth). It was five storeys in height with four rooms wainscotted and four rooms wainscotted half-way. It has one portland stone chimney piece (only those of portland stone or marble were mentioned). The building, having been damaged in the disastrous fire of March 1748, was destroyed in the fire of 1759 which swept Cornhill, a detailed description of which can be found in the *Gentleman's Magazine* for that year. Edward Vaughan then moved with his family to number 6, St Michael's Alley, next to St Michael's Churchyard. The new premises formed the southern end of the Jamaica Coffee House and adjoined on the other side the George and Vulture. The deeds still survive and these show a frontage of seventeen feet five inches and a depth of thirty-two feet nine inches.

It is difficult to know what Edward Vaughan was like as a person. There is a note in the front of the Fan-Makers Company's Stamp Book that he was serving on the Court of Assistants in 1749, the date the book was commenced, so that it is almost certain he went on to serve as Warden and Master if he was not already a Past Master by this date (unfortunately the Minute Books and other Company records for this period which could have established this are lost).

A letter in the Heal Collection in the British Museum refers to a fine trade card of his dating from *c* 1740 formerly pasted in a Hogarth tome in the Dyson Perring Collection at Malvern, but it has proved impossible to trace.

He had two recorded apprentices, Elizabeth Ebbett, daughter of Samuel Ebbett who paid a premium of £6 in 1740, and Mary Kitchin, £10.10.0 in 1755. It would appear from a biographical account in the *Hibernian Magazine*, October 1804, that William Vaughan was also brought up in his elder brother's business of fan painting before deciding to go on the stage. It is known that Edward was in the habit of selling tickets each year for Hannah Pritchard's Benefits as the name 'Mr Vaughan Fanmaker at the Golden Fan next the Royal Exchange Cornhill' often appears on her playbills advertising these. His name and that of his widow Amy Ann annually recur in the Drury Lane Account Books so that it is highly likely he supplied the Theatre with costume fans.

One imagines he would not have been slow to take advantage of his stage connections and no doubt he did a lavish trade—theatrical fans showing scenes from the popular plays of the day, particularly those in which his famous sister was best known. Many such fans have survived, but as they are rarely, if ever, signed it is almost impossible to identify them as the works of a particular maker.

James Lynch in his book *Box, Pit and Gallery* makes the interesting observation that because of the moral stigma attached to the stage and its players, ladies in the later seventeenth century were expected to attend the theatre wearing masks. Some of this attitude remained well into the next century, and indeed until the 1760s, in spite of the claims of Collier, Cibber and Steele to have reformed the stage 'so that fashionable accoutrements that could represent ritualistic moral objection without hindering the enjoyment of the drama were still necessary.' The fan simply took the place of the mask—and 'had the advantage of being able to disguise the blush (or its absence) without concealing its owner's identity.'

Edward's name constantly recurs also in the Vestry Minutes and Church Wardens' Accounts for St Michael, Cornhill, where he served as Church Warden, sidesman, auditor of accounts and, for very many years, overseer of the poor. He was also a collector of land tax, for Thomas Lennard in his will mentions having stood surety for him.

He married Amy Ann Gilbert. They had two sons, Thomas Lennard (1743–78) and Edward (1746–c 1814). Both boys were scholars of St Paul's School, Thomas being admitted in 1754 and Edward in 1755. Thomas was commissioned in the Royal Artillery, having entered the Royal Military Academy, Woolwich, as a cadet in 1760, and was killed in action in the war of American Independence at the Battle of the Court House, Monmouth, New Jersey, during the British retreat from Philadelphia on 28th June, 1778. He died unmarried and is mentioned in Major Duncan's *History of the Royal Artillery*.

Edward, the younger son, was a miniature painter and exhibited regularly at the Society of Artists and later the Royal Academy over a period of some forty years. He married Sarah King, a Huguenot girl from Christchurch, Spitalfields, at St Michael, Cornhill, on 29th May, 1773. Her uncle was William Jourdain the Silk Mercer, whose shop in Artillery Row, just off Bishopsgate, is said to have the finest mid-Georgian shop front still surviving in London.

After Edward the Fanmaker's death on the morning of Friday 21st March, 1766, 'of an apoplectick fit' according to the contemporary newspapers, his widow Amy Ann kept on the fanmaking business, assisted by her two spinster daughters Amy Ann (1741–1826) and Henrietta (1739–98). For the remainder of her long life—she died in 1799 at the age of 95—she also held the appointments of Sextoness and Organ Blower to the Church of St Michael, Cornhill. On her death, her surviving daughter Amy Ann succeeded to the appointments in her place and continued as Sextoness and Organ Blower until her death in 1826. She continued to live at 6, St Michael's Alley and apparently to practise as a fanmaker—she was certainly still in business there in 1820.

This meticulously researched account of the lives of one fan-maker's family is invaluable in helping to piece together the working lives of fanmakers in the eighteenth and early nineteenth centuries, and shows how they took part in their local community of church and theatre. It is also of interest to follow the continuity of fanmaking and the protection they must have been accorded by their Guild, the powerful Worshipful Company of Fan-Makers.

7 Present-Day Collectors

Some well-known collections of fine fans were made during the nineteenth century and the first half of the twentieth. One early name was that of Robert Walker: his collection was catalogued for his exhibition at the Fine Arts Society in 1882. Lady Charlotte Schrieber was another and her collection was catalogued by Lionel Cust when she gave the majority of her fans to the British Museum in 1891. The Messel Collection was formed early in the twentieth century by Colonel Leonard Messel (now owned by his daughter Anne, Countess of Rosse) together with the De Witt Clinton Cohen Collection which formed the nucleus of the Oldham Collection. Three other collections of note are the Rothschild Collection at Waddesden Manor, the Bristol Collection at Ickworth and Felix Tal's Collection in Amsterdam.

On the whole there was very little interest in fans during the years 1930 to 1970. No books were written about them in English and, because there was simply no market for them, some fans changed hands for a few pence. A fine fan might be sold at a famous auction house sale but within the category 'toys' or 'costume', never in a category of its own.

Eventually, in 1974, a trio of fan enthusiasts became friendly collaborators, the catalyst being a private lecture given by the author at the Victoria and Albert Museum to a most distinguished international audience: the subject was 'The Messel Collection of Fans'. This was given in the same year as *A Collector's History of Fans* was published, the first of the new crop of books on fans.

An Englishman, Martin Willcocks, suggested to the author the idea of a society for fan collectors and they both invited Mrs Hélène Alexander to join them. For almost a year the groundwork for such a club was explored, opinions asked, affiliations tentatively suggested and feelers put out into both the museum and collectors' worlds. Was the fan art or craft? Should we 'tag on' to an established organisation or branch out into the unknown?

Eventually it was agreed that our aim was to establish a society based on a serious pursuit of academic knowledge, yet we should never lose interest in the fact that we were collectors first and foremost and that any society should be fun, too! It seemed clear that there was a need for some authoritative body which would work at a very high level through museums, art galleries, textile and costume societies and the like and, especially, should learn from the age-old Worshipful Company of Fan-Makers—the only fan City and Craft Guild in the world still in existence. Therefore a wide spectrum was envisaged in order to bring in established as well as would-be collectors, staff of museums, art historians, those interested in ethnography, Orientalists and those working in the conservation field.

In 1975 the Fan Circle was born. At a later date the name was altered to the Fan Circle International (because so many members joined from all over the world) and in 1982 the FCI was registered as a Charity, mainly for educational purposes.

Patrons were invited to enhance the FCI with their names and, to everyone's delight and benefit, each agreed and all have been much more than names on FCI stationery.

It seemed only right to invite the annually elected Master of the Fan-Makers to be a patron, and gradually a solidifying relationship is being established with this generous Livery Company. In Britain two patrons were invited, a famous collector and a famous authority on costume: Anne, Countess of Rosse (owner of the Messel Collection) and Mrs Doris Langley-Moore, originator of the Costume Museum in Bath. From the United States the FCI enticed Miss Esther Oldham, the great authority and also the owner of the Oldham Collection, and from Europe Mr Felix Tal from Amsterdam. All these patrons have taken a keen interest in the FCI, helping whenever and wherever they can, setting a tone and standard of excellence. As a 'badge' for their initiative the three innovators were, in 1982, made honorary members of the FCI.

The magnet which attracts members of any society is the written word. For FCI members that is the *FCI Bulletin*, made up of at least 38 printed pages (A4 size), published three times a year. With hindsight it is noticeable how carefully the balance has been controlled to provide original research, advertisements, illustrations, advance news of auction sales (London and occasionally elsewhere) followed by an analysis of each sale—including (fearless) comment on both prices and quality—letters and news from members, articles, advance notice of events and analytical reports on them afterwards.

Another important function of the FCI is its mounting and promotion of exhibitions. On each occasion the FCI has worked in harmonious friendship with the staff of the museum involved, with co-operation all along the line. The FCI has solicited the fans from a variety of sources, together with the captions for the catalogues, and assisted in the mounting of the exhibits under the skill of Hélène Alexander.

The first of the FCI exhibitions was called 'The World of the Fan' and was seen at the Harris Museum of Art in Preston, Lancashire, in 1976.

The second, 'Fans from the East', was displayed first in 1978 at the City Museum and Art Gallery in Birmingham, and then in 1979 at the Victoria and Albert Museum in London.

The third exhibition, 'Fans and the Grand Tour' was held in 1982/3 at the Museum in Brighton. Both the first and the third had their own catalogues, but, because the second differed in size from Birmingham to London, it was made the subject of a book, published by Debrett, giving much original material on this largely unknown subject.

With such a run of specialised exhibitions set up by international academics, it must come as no surprise to learn that two further subjects are already on the drawingboard for the very near future, and, hopefully, the torch will carry on from hand to hand.

Gradually the 1975 aims are being achieved, consciously much broader than a mere society for collectors. The FCI is now considered the world authority on the subject, having developed an intellectual responsibility and always speaking with an informed voice. In time it is hoped to establish its own premises, show fans, get together a world bibliography, have established archives (already quite large), a collection of specialist books and catalogues and a photographic library, be able to advise about places in various countries were fans might be seen or bought, and to give specialist advice on both the conservation and renovation of fans.

The purposes of the FCI are eminently worthy and the list of its achievements quite astonishing for such a short period. What is also remarkable about the organisation is the spectrum of its members:

many men amongst the women, both established collectors and absolute beginners with only a handful of fans, but, in every case, apparently fascinated with the subject.

Until the FCI acquires its own premises, interested readers may make contact through the following address: The Hon. Secretary, Fan Circle International, 24 Asmuns Hill, Hampstead Garden Suburb, London NW11 6ET.

In the United States there was formerly the highly academic Fan Guild of Boston, Massachusetts, sadly disbanded some years ago. Then a group of enthusiasts in San Francisco launched the East Bay Fan Guild and, in 1982, another organisation was founded called FANA (Fan Association of North America). Distances are so great in the United States that it must be unbearably tantalising to read of social events in the United Kingdom which they cannot attend, for the most important requirement for collectors is that they should not be banished to a vacuum: they must be allowed to meet and discuss their own collections as often as is feasible. Real enthusiasts belong to every organisation, so that everyone is able to contribute something of interest and no one suffers a feeling of isolation. Let us hope that in the future members of each of the above organisations (as well as others in Australia, and throughout the world) will be able to travel to each other on a regular basis, especially for seminars (such as the one in Dieppe in 1982) and to enjoy exhibitions.

49. French fan, the leaf painted with a lady, her admirer, and putti, signed by A. Solde: the ivory sticks pierced and gilt, the guards set with silver-gilt and turquoises and split pearls, signed Wiese (being a French jeweller who exhibited in the 1862 Exhibition). 11″: 28 cms. c 1865. By courtesy of Christies, South Kensington.

Bibliography

ALEXANDER, HÉLÈNE. 'German Fan Fair', article in *Art & Antiques Weekly*, May 1980.

ALEXANDER, HÉLÈNE. 'Some Facets of Fan Collecting, Part One: The Finer Examples', article in *Antique Collecting*, Dec. 1979.

ALEXANDER, HÉLÈNE. 'The Pleasures of Fans', article in *Apollo*, 1977.

ARMSTRONG, NANCY. *Abanicos*, (translated by Juan Costa) Castell Ediciones, S.A., Barcelona, 1979.

ARMSTRONG, NANCY. *A Collector's History of Fans*, Studio Vista, London, and Clarkson N. Potter, Inc., New York, 1974.

ARMSTRONG, NANCY. 'Fans from the Seychelles to the Philippines', article in *Country Life*, 1978.

ARMSTRONG, NANCY. *Jewellery: An Historical Survey of British Styles and Jewels*, Lutterworth Press, Guildford, 1973.

ARMSTRONG, NANCY. 'Regency Horn Fans', article in *The Antique Collector*, 1978.

ARMSTRONG, NANCY. *The Book of Fans*, Colour Library International, New Malden, and Mayflower Books, New York, 1978.

ARMSTRONG, NANCY. *Victorian Jewellery*, Studio Vista, London, and Macmillan, New York, 1976.

Art Journal. *Catalogue of the 1851 Exhibition*.

Arundel Society. *Fans of All Countries*, 1871.

BADEN-POWELL, B. H. *Handbook of the Manufactures and Arts of the Punjab*, 1872.

BAPST, GERMAIN. *Deux Éventails du Musée de Louvre*, Paris, 1882.

BARO, CARLOS M., and ESCODA, JUAN. *Éventails Anciens*, Payot, Lausanne, 1957. (Also under *Alte Fächer*, showing collection from Barcelona).

BENNETT, ANNA G., and BERSON, RUTH. *Fans in Fashion*, Catalogue of the Exhibition, San Francisco, 1981.

BERKHOUT, J. G. *Waaierweelde in Beeckestijn keuze uit het waaierkabinet*

Felix Tal, Exhibition Catalogue, 1979.

BLONDEL, M. S. *History of Fans*, Librairie Renouard, Paris, 1875.

BLONDEL, M. S. *Histoire des Éventails chez tous les Peuples et à toutes les Époques*, Librairie Renouard, Paris, 1875.

BOEHN, MAX VON. *Accessorias de la Moda*, Salvar Editores S. A., Barcelona–Buenos Aires, 1944.

BOGER, H. BATERSON. *The Traditional Arts of Japan*, Doubleday, New York, 1964.

BORDEILLES, PIERRE DE, SEIGNEUR DE BRANTOME. *Memoires des dames illustrée de France*.

BOUCHOT, HENRI. 'L'Histoire par les Éventails Populaires', two articles in *Les Lettres et Les Arts*, Paris, 1883.

BOWIE, HENRY P. *On the Laws of Japanese Painting*, Paul Elder, San Francisco, 1941.

BUSH, GEORGE. *Der Fächer*, Dusseldorf, 1904.

CATALINI, CARLA. *Waaiers*, Van Dishoeck, Bussom, Holland, 1966.

Catalogue of the Celebrated Collection of Fans of Mr. Robert Walker— exhibited at the Fine Art Society's, 148 New Bond Street, London, 1882.

Catholic Encyclopaedia, The. Vol. 6, article on flabelli, Caxton, London & New York 1909–1912.

CHIBA, REIKO. *Painted Fans of Japan: 15 Noh Drama Masterpieces*, Tuttle & Co., Rutland, Vermont, and Tokyo, Japan, 1962.

COLLINS, BERNARD ROSS. *A Short Account of the Worshipful Company of Fan-Makers*, Favel Press, London, 1950.

COOMARASWAMY, A. K. *Arts and Crafts of India and Ceylon*, 1913.

COSWAY, M. 'English Fans', article in *The Concise Encyclopaedia of Antiques IV*, 1959.

CROFT-MURRAY, EDWARD. 'Watteau's Design for a Fan Leaf', article in *Apollo*, 1974.

CROSSMAN, CARL L. *The China Trade*, Princeton, 1972.

CUNNINGTON, C. W. and R. E., and BEARD, CHARLES. *A Dictionary of English Costume 900–1900*, A. & C. Black, London, 1960.

CUST, LIONEL. *Catalogue of the Collection of Fans and Fan Leaves presented to the Trustees of the British Museum by Lady Charlotte Schrieber*, Longmans, London, 1893.

DAWES, LEONARD. 'The Nicely Calculated Flutter of the Fan', article in *Antique Dealer and Collectors Guide*, March, 1974.

DUNN, D. 'On Fans', article in *The Connoisseur*, 1902.

DUVAL, E. *Les éventails*, Paris, 1885.

DUVELLEROY. 'Exposition Universelle, Paris 1867', in *Rapports du Jury International Vol. IV*.

EEGHEN, DR. I. H. VAN. *De Amsterdamse Waaierindustrie, ae XVIIIe eeuw, Amstelodamum*, 1953.

EEGHEN, DR. I. H. VAN. *Tijdschrift voor Geschiedenis*, Amsterdam, 1961.

EITNER, LORENZ E. A. *The Flabellum of Tournus*, College of Art Association of America, sponsored by the Archeological Institute of America, 1941.

Enciclopedia Universal Illustrada—Europeo Americana, Madrid.

ERLER, M. *Der Moderne Fächer*, Kunstgewerbeblatt, 1904.

Fan Circle International, The, and Brighton Museum. *Fans and the Grand Tour*, Catalogue of the Exhibition, 1982/3.

Fan Circle International, The, and the Harris Museum and Art Gallery, Preston. *The World of the Fan*, Catalogue of the Exhibition, 1976.

Fan Circle International publications (including *Bulletins*) 1975–1983.

Fans from the East, various authors, Debrett's Peerage in association with the Fan Circle International and the Victoria and Albert Museum, London, 1978.

Fan Leaves, published by The Fan Guild, Boston, Mass., U.S.A., 1961.

FLORY, M. A. *A Book About Fans*, Macmillan & Co., New York, 1895.

FOWLES, W. A. *The Revised History of the Worshipful Company of Fan-Makers 1709–1975*, Lund Humphries, Bradford and London, 1977.

GALTER, JUAN SUBIAS. *El Arte Popular en España*, Editorial Seix Barral, S.A., Barcelona, 1948.

GIBSON, EUGENIE. 'Queen Mary's Collection', article in *The Connoisseur*, 1927.

GIBSON, EUGENIE. 'The Golden Age of the Fan', article in *The Connoisseur*, 1920.

GILCHRIST, JAMES. *Anglican Church Plate*, The Connoisseur and Michael Joseph, London, 1967.

GILES, H. A. 'Chinese Fans', article in *Fraser's Magazine*, London, May, 1879.

GINSBURG, MADELEINE. *Victorian Dress in Photography*, Batsford, London, 1983.

GOSSON, STEPHEN. *Pleasant Quippes for Upstart Newfangled Gentlewomen*, London, 1596.

GOSTELOW, MARY. *The Fan*, Gill & Macmillan, Dublin, 1976.

Great Exhibition, The, Official Catalogue of, London, 1851.

GREEN, BERTHA DE VERE. *A Collector's Guide to Fans over the Ages*, Muller, London, 1975.

GROS, GABRIELLA. 'The Art of the Fanmaker,' article in *Apollo*, 1957.

HAMMAR, BRITTA. (Swedish) *Fans of the 18th century*, Kulturen 1976, translated by Marion Maule for the *FCI Newsletter/Bulletin*.

HEATH, RICHARD. 'Politics in dress', article in *The Woman's World*, June, 1889.

HENDERSON, MILNE. Catalogue of the Exhibition *The Art of Chinese Fan Painting*, London, 1974.

HENDERSON, MILNE. Catalogue of the Exhibition *Nanga Fan Painting*, London, 1975.

HIRSHORN, A. A. 'Mourning Fans', article in *Antiques*, 1973.

HOLME, C. 'Modern Design in Jewellery and Fans', article in *Studio*, 1902.

HOLT, T. H. 'On Fans, their use and antiquity', *Journal of the British Archaeological Association*, 1870.

HONOUR, HUGH. *Chinoiserie: The Vision of Cathay*, John Murray, London, 1961.

Household Guide, The, Vol. 1. Cassells, London, 1880.

HUGHES, THERLE. 'A Flutter of Fans', article in *Discovering Antiques*, London, 1971.

HUGHES, THERLE. 'Fans from the Leonard Messel Collection', two articles in *Country Life*, June, 1972.

HUGHES, THERLE. *More Small Decorative Antiques*, Lutterworth Press, London, 1962.

HUGHES, THERLE. 'Storm Dragons and Plum Blossom', article in *Country Life*, 1972.

HUTH, HANS. *Lacquer of the West: The History of a Craft and an Industry, 1550–1950*, Chicago, 1971.

IMPEY, O. *Chinoiserie: The Impact of Oriental Styles on Western Art and Decoration*, London, 1977.

IRÖNS, NEVILLE J. *Fans of Imperial China*, Kaiserreich Kunst (Hong Kong) and The House of Fans, London, 1982.

IRÖNS, NEVILLE J. *Fans of Imperial Japan*, Kaiserreich Kunst (Hong Kong) and The House of Fans, London, 1982.

JACKSON, MRS F. NEVILL. 'The Montgolfiers', article in *The Connoisseur*, 1909.

JENYNS, SOANE. *A Background to Chinese Painting*, London, 1935.

JOURDAIN, M., AND JENYNS, S. *Chinese Export Art in the Eighteenth Century*, London, 1950.

KENDALL, B. 'CONCERNING FANS', article in *The Connoisseur*, 1903.

KIYOE, NAKAMURA. *Nihon no Ogi (Fans of Japan)*, Oyashima Shuppan, Kyoto, 1942.

KIYOE, NAKAMURA. *Ogi to Ogie (Fans and Fan Painting)*, Kawara Shoten, Kyoto, 1969.

LEARY, E. *Fans in Fashion*, Catalogue of the Exhibition, Temple Newsam, Leeds, 1975.

Leisure Hour, The, London, 1882.

L'ESTOILE, PIERRE DE. *The Isle of the Hermaphrodites*, 1588.

Liverpool Arts Club, *Exhibition Catalogue*, 1877.

MARCEL, GABRIEL. *En Éventail Historique du dix-huitieme Siècle*, Paris, 1901.

MARGARY, IVAN D. 'Militia Camps in Sussex, 1793, and a Lady's Fan', Sussex Archaeological Records, Vd 107, 1969.

MAYOR, SUSAN. *Collecting Fans*, Studio Vista, London, 1980.

MELLING, JOHN K. *Discovering London's Guilds and Liveries*, Shire Publications Ltd., Aylesbury, 1981.

'Milady's Fan—500 years of a Coy History', article in *Majorca Daily Bulletin*, 1970.

MONGOT, VINCENTO ALMELA. *Los Abanicos (Fans of Valencia)*, Spain.

MONTGOMERY, MARY C. 'Fan Histories and Fashions', article in *The Cosmopolitan*, 1890.

MOTOI, OI. *Instructions in Sumi Painting*, Tokyo, 1958.

MOUREY, GABRIEL (with others). *Art Nouveau Jewellery and Fans*, Dover Publications, New York, 1973.

MUNSTERBERG, HUGO. *The Landscape Painting of China and Japan*, Tuttle & Co., Rutland, Vermont, 1955.

New Encyclopaedia Britannica, The (30 vols), 1974.

NEWTON, STELLA M. *Renaissance Theatre Costume*, Rapp and Whiting, 1975.

NIVEN, T. *The Fan in Art*, New York, 1911.

NORITAKE, TSUDA. *Ideals of Japanese Painting*, Tokyo, 1958.

OHM, DR. ANNALIESE. *Fächer, Reallexikon zur Deutschen Kunstgeschichte*, Stuttgart, 1972.

OLDHAM, ESTHER. 'Fans of the Paper Stainers: Dominotier and

Imagier', article in *Hobbies*, December, 1959.

OLDHAM, ESTHER. 'Jenny Lind', article in *Antiques Journal*, November, 1961.

OLDHAM, ESTHER. 'Mrs Jack's Fans', article in *Spinning Wheel,* May, 1967.

OLDHAM, ESTHER. 'The Fan. A Gentleman's Accessory', article in *The Connoisseur* 125:14–20.

PALLISER, MRS BURY. *History of Lace*, 1865.

PARR, LOUISA. 'The Fan', article in *Harper's Magazine*, London, August, 1889.

PERCIVAL, MACIVER. 'Some Old English Printed Paper Fans', article in *The Connoisseur* 44, p 141.

PERCIVAL, MACIVER. *The Fan Book*, Fisher Unwin, London, 1920.

PERIS-MENCHETA, JUAN. *Libros y Abanicos*, Barcelona, 1946.

PETIT, EDOUARD. *Etudes, Souvenirs et Considérations sur le fabrication de l'éventail*, Versailles, 1859.

REDGRAVE, S. *Catalogue of the Loan Exhibition of Fans*, South Kensington Museum, 1870.

RHEAD, GEORGE WOOLISCROFT. *History of the Fan*, Kegan Paul, Trench, Trubner & Co., London, 1910.

REIG Y FLORES. *La Industria Abaniquera en Valencia*, Tipografía de Archivos, Madrid, 1933.

ROBINSON, F. MABEL. 'Fans', article in *The Woman's World*, London, January, 1889.

ROCAMORA, MANUEL. *Abanicos Históricos y Anecdóticos*, Tobella, Barcelona, 1956.

ROSENBERG, MARC. *Alte und Neue Fächer aus dem Wettbewerbung und Ausstellung zu Karlsruhe*, Vienna, 1891.

RUSSELL, RONALD. *Discovering Antique Prints*, Shire Publications Ltd., Aylesbury, 1982.

SALWEY, CHARLOTTE MARIA (née Birch). *Fans of Japan*, Kegan, Paul, Trench, Trubner & Co., London, 1894. And her private book of Press Cuttings lent to me by her grand-daughter, Mrs Anne Wright.

SCHAFER, EDWARD H. *The Golden Peaches of Samarkand*, California, 1963.

SCHRIEBER, LADY CHARLOTTE. *Fans and Fan Leaves—English*, John Murray, London, 1888.

SCHRIEBER, LADY CHARLOTTE. *Fans and Fan Leaves—Foreign*, John Murray, London, 1890.

Sheppard, Mubin. *Taman Indera* (Malay Decorative Arts and Pastimes), 1971.

Sociedad Española de Amigos del Arte. *El Abanico en España,* Madrid, June, 1920.

Spielmann, Heinz. *Oskar Kokoscha: die Fächer für Alma Mahler,* Verlag Hans Christians, Hamburg, 1969.

Standen, Edith A. 'Instruments for Agitating the Air', article in the *Metropolitan Museum of Art,* New York, 1965.

Strange, Edward F. *The Colour-Prints of Hiroshige,* Cassell & Co., London, 1925.

Taipei, Taiwan. *Masterpieces of Chinese Album Painting in the National Palace Museum,* 1971.

Tal, Felix. *De Waaier Collectie Felix Tal,* (Exhibition in Utrecht, 1967).

Thornton, Peter. 'Fans', article in *Antiques International,* London, 1966.

University of Kansas. *Chinese Fan Paintings from the Collection of Mr Chan Yee-Pong,* Lawrence, Kansas, 1971.

Uzanne, Octave. *The Fan,* Nimmo and Bain, London, 1884.

Van Briessen, Fritz. *The Way of the Brush,* Tuttle & Co., Rutland, Vermont and Tokyo.

Vaughan, Anthony. *Born to Please. Hannah Pritchard, Actress, 1711–1768, A Critical Biography,* The Society for Theatre Research, London, 1979.

Viften— The Fan, Catalogue of the Exhibition in Copenhagen, 1957.

Waddell, Madeleine C. 'The Rise and Fall of the Fan', article in *The Antique Collector,* December, 1966.

Wardle, Patricia. 'Two Late Nineteenth Century Lace Fans', article in *Embroidery* 1970.

White, Margaret E. 'Collecting Handscreens', article in *Antiques,* April, 1941.

Woman's World, article on fans, London, 1889.

Yee, Chiang. *The Chinese Eye,* London, 1935.

Yetts, W. P. *Symbolism in Chinese Art,* Leyden, 1912.

Zauber des Fächers: Fächer aus dem Besitz des Museums, Altonaer Museum, Hamburg, 1974.

Index